Roses in a F(

A Holocaust Love Story

By Elise Garibaldi

Copyright © 2016 by Elise Garibaldi

www.elisegaribaldi.com

All rights reserved. Published by Decalogue Books. This book may not be reproduced, in whole or in part, in any form without express permission from the author.

Library of Congress Cataloging-in-Publication Data Garibaldi, Elise, 2015

Roses in a Forbidden Garden by Elise Garibaldi

1. Holocaust. 2. Theresienstadt/Terezín. 3. German Jews. 4. Bremen.

FRONT COVER: Inge Katz at 17 years of age

Dedication

In Loving Memory of

Ruthie Cohen, Rosa Gruenberg, Carl Katz,
Marianne (Gruenberg) Katz, Sam (Schmuel) Berger

Contents

Theresienstadt November 11, 1943 5
November 9, 1938 A Beautiful Life Shattered 7
Shards of Glass 23
Deportation 35
Last Transports Out of Bremen 49
Arbeit Macht Frei (Work Will Set You Free) 61
Schmuel 81
The Red Cross Will Save Us 93
Roses in a Forbidden Garden 105
We Will Never Be Separated 117
Branded Inmates 125
Machine Guns in the Night 131
From One Hell to Another 139
The Gates are Opened 151
Last Night in Dachau 157
Returning to "Normal" 165
Dachau's Liberators 177
Where Is He? 189
Acknowledgments 204

Theresienstadt
November 11, 1943

"Just get it over with already," Inge murmured to herself as she stared at the rising sun that rainy morning. She couldn't bear to hear her mother sobbing like that any longer—nor could she stand how cruelly the elderly and weak were being treated. How inhumane to force them to stand out in the open for hours on end. The Germans counted, recounted, and counted again. Hour after hour they were forced to remain on their feet in orderly rows and given nothing to eat or drink. Inge's feet ached, and her back pained her. But what could they do with all those rifles aimed directly at them?

    As the sun started to set, and darkness approached, she couldn't help but notice how clear the night sky had become. She could see the stars; there were so many right over their heads. It helped her to remember that there was a bigger and better world out there. Behind the high walls surrounding the ghetto, and all the restricting barbed wire, she could catch a glimpse of the rolling hills. Yes, past the rifles ready to shoot her in the back if she were to try running away, there was indeed a bigger world. She could sense that it was orderly, beautiful, and peaceful. It was possible for her to dream of Schmuel and of the marigold. That flower, she understood, he had given to her was meant not only as a birthday present but as a message from G-d that she was destined to love and be loved. In that moment, she was able to forget about her aching feet and sore back, even about the sobbing women and the wavering elderly. She focused all her energy on how to search for him, for Schmuel.

Chapter One

November 9, 1938
A Beautiful Life Shattered

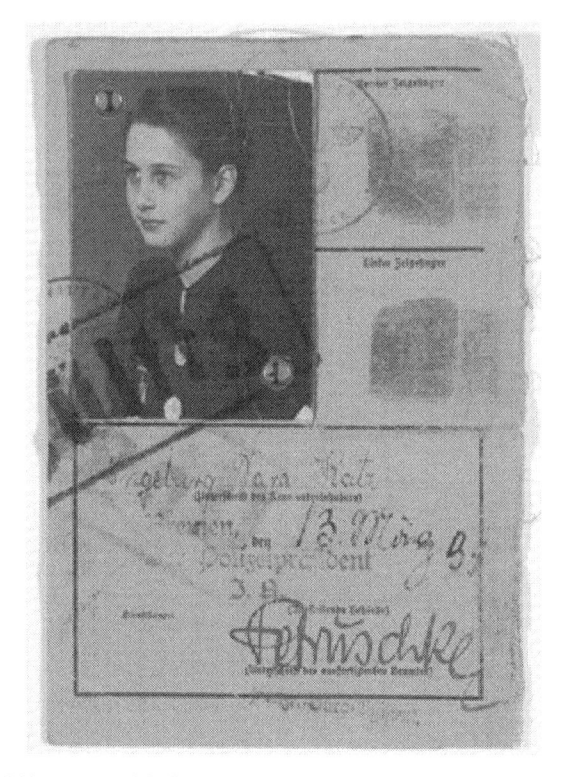

Inge "Sara" Katz, age 13. The Nazis added the middle name of "Sara" on all passports and other official papers to identify any woman as being Jewish.

Inge, the daughter of Carl Katz, a successful businessman in Bremen, Germany, had been disciplined from an early age not only to be respectful but well-mannered. That meant it was imperative for her to always be groomed and properly put together—but never to draw too much attention to herself.

Often dressed in pleated skirts and woolen sweaters, she'd only roll her long woolen socks down below her knees when she was away from her parents' authoritative eyes.

Her thick hair was worn straight, extending below her jawline, and her sparkling green eyes radiated in sharp contrast with her dark hair. The year was 1938, and, at fourteen years of age, she was already several inches taller than her mother. Sitting now at her grandmother's bedroom vanity, she loved to use Oma's (German for grandma) silver brush to comb her hair back behind her ears. Sometimes she'd even spritz some of her grandmother's 4711 cologne on her neck and wrists.

Having completed her efforts to make herself pretty, Inge got up from the upholstered stool accompanying the vanity to look out the window and observe the pedestrian traffic on the street below. The Katz family was living in her grandmother's home, which was less than a twenty-minute walk from the cobblestoned center of Bremen, a city not far from the North Sea. She loved to watch the bustle on weekday mornings. It was still an era when women didn't leave home without wearing a hat. She noted the men rushing by to get to work on time. It was autumn, and on such a brisk morning, everyone held their hats with one hand against the oncoming winds and kept their overcoats closed with the other.

The delivery boy from the local bakery, about to remount his bicycle, was making his way from their front door and walking along the path to the iron gate leading to the street. Inge loved the smell of the freshly baked rolls delivered by these boys each morning in their small canvas knapsacks. As she made her way out the door of her bedroom she shared with her grandmother to join her family downstairs around the breakfast table, the smells of coffee brewing and warm milk were already wafting up the stairwell to greet her.

Her father, as she reached the table, was quickly finishing off a soft-boiled egg, all the while being careful not to get any spots on his tie as he dunked a piece of bread into it. Vati (German for dad) was a handsome man, Inge thought, as she gazed at him in his well-tailored gray suit. During World War I, then known as the Great War, over twenty years earlier, he had served Germany as a young soldier. Those years of training and combat had left him with an athletic and strong frame. He had classic even features, with a strong commanding jawline, which had served to intimidate more than a few men. But his large, flashing blue eyes could also evince much laughter and mischief. Inge doubted whether anyone would deny him any request when confronted with such wicked charms. She laughed to herself—at least she and her mother certainly couldn't. Vati took one last sip of coffee and placed a hurried kiss upon Inge's forehead. After a brief reminder from him that she must mind her elders, Mutti (German for mom) walked him to the door. A faint smell of tobacco and aftershave lingered in the air behind him as he made his way out.

Even at this early hour, Inge's mother was already wearing heels and had her hair freshly set into a wavy bob. For years, she had been tying her long brown hair into a knot behind her head. But her recent, then fashionable, haircut left Inge's father disappointed. She was a woman who religiously kept an eye on the latest styles and adapted them to suit herself. Mutti was of slight proportions, and she prided herself on her ability to maintain a tiny waistline after so many years. One wouldn't call her beautiful, but she had fine, pleasant-looking features, and most everyone would say she was pretty. Marianne always knew how to put herself together in ways that could make heads turn when she entered a room.

As soon as her father left home that morning, Inge, too, wished she still had a school to attend. But, after Hitler's Nuremberg Laws of 1935 stripped German Jews of their citizenship, the expulsion of all Jewish children from the public schools began in earnest. Inge and her cousin Ruthie had been the only Jewish children in their class at the Delmestrasse School. Even then, because they were Jewish, they were forced to sit in the last row. Whenever the principal spoke to the class on how despicable the Jews were, she felt ashamed. He described how they would lie in coffins in their social clubs and cheat and steal from others. Inge never found anything that was even conceivably true in his rants, but she was too fearful to even dream of correcting him. Instead, she and Ruthie just sat quietly in their seats, hoping not to draw attention to themselves.

But it seemed that everyone in her class turned and looked at them somewhat fearfully after these talks. It appeared, however, that even the principal had trouble lumping Inge and Ruthie with the rest of their "sick and malevolent race" because, before turning the class back to the teacher, he would at times remark that, "This doesn't mean that Inge and Ruthie are bad, though."

One thing she was glad not to do because she was no longer in school was to swear her allegiance to a flag with a swastika upon it every school day. Oftentimes, she felt like not saluting the flag, but the fear of the repercussions for such behavior scared her into submission. Now, with no longer having to rush off to school in the morning, she helped clear the table of the breakfast dishes and then performed other daily chores about the house.

Her grandmother's home was quite large but nonetheless manageable. It was a pretty, two-storied house with white-painted window frames. Rose bushes, both red and yellow, stood in the front yard. It was situated at #33 Isarstrasse in one of the nice sections of Bremen. Inge and her parents had moved there several months earlier shortly after her grandfather's passing. Her family thought it would be the best way to care for Oma. Because Grandma Rosa was such a sweet and kind woman, it didn't bother Inge very much, even being assigned to share her grandmother's room, including the same bed.

Among Inge's tasks was to polish the bronze fixtures on the outside of their home: the doorknobs, mailbox slot, and the faucet used to water plants in the garden. Upon completing that job, Inge then went over to the bench in the front facing the yard and the street beyond to sweep away the fallen leaves. You never knew when one of her relatives who lived within walking distance might stop by for tea. They would sit with her parents while she and her cousin Ruthie played some game, like hopscotch or catch. Neighborhood children also used to stop by. But by then, it had been some time since any of them had been allowed to pay a visit to a Jewish household.

The morning on that day seemed to be passing quickly. Inge had to be sure to grab her jacket, given the weather, and the lunch her mother prepared for her if she were to make it in time to meet Ruthie at the nearby tramway stop. Inge ran part of the way to Meterstrasse, where she found Ruthie already waiting for her. It would take the girls a good half hour before they could reach Bremen's Schwachausen District, but it was enough time to chat and giggle on the tram before their serious work for the day would begin.

They quickly jumped off the tram at the Hartwigstrasse stop and walked several blocks to the elegant and stately home of Frau Herzberg. She was a refined German woman who owned an exclusive Atelier, which catered to Bremen's upscale women. Inge's grandmother and mother were among those who frequented this shop, which is how Inge had come to know this most unusual woman. Frau Herzberg wasn't Jewish but had taken pity on Inge and her cousin when she learned that the Nazi regime no longer permitted Jewish children to attend public school. Married to a Jewish man herself, but with no children of her own, she did her best to help others in the only way she knew how: by offering girls like Inge and Ruthie apprenticeships.

Inge reveled in the day-to-day routine, as she felt fortunate to be able to learn this trade. Just seven months into her two- year apprenticeship, she looked forward to the time when she would be customizing dresses for her own clientele. At her present stage, though, she was restricted to just observing pattern-making techniques, using only basic hand-stitching, and conducting preliminary fittings. Still, it did not stop her from fantasizing about the time when she would one day open up an Atelier of her own with Ruthie. They had even selected a name for it: Katz & Co, after their respective last names of Katz and Cohen.

When the last client of the day finished admiring herself in one of Frau Herzberg's custom-made outfits in the three-way mirror on the main floor, Inge was pleased to hear that the lady was satisfied and would be taking the garment home with her. Besides, she was getting tired, and it was getting late. Moreover, each successive November evening was becoming dark earlier and earlier, and it was getting increasingly cold.

After they swept the workroom and scoured every inch of the basement shop floor with horseshoe magnets to collect fallen needles, the cousins removed the pincushions from about their wrists and placed them back at their workstations for the next day. Little did they realize, however, that this would be the very last time they would ever be walking up that stairway. After asking Frau Herzberg's permission to leave, and having asserted that not a single needle was missing, the girls made their trip home for dinner.

As soon as Inge passed through the gate leading to the front path of Oma's house and mounted the black-and-white tiled steps just outside the front door, she was embraced with the aroma of a stew her mother and grandmother had been cooking. A large pot, simmering on the stove in the kitchen, was filled to the brim with beans, potatoes, and chunks of lamb. Her grandmother was putting down her tasting spoon and contemplating whether more salt was needed. The mere aroma of the food was enough to cause hunger pangs in Inge's stomach. Right after Mutti greeted her with a warm smile, she immediately told her daughter to set the table right after she hung up her coat.

It was so good to sit with her entire family in that dining room, as each retold what had transpired that day. Grandma Rosa then inquired about her friend, Frau Herzberg.

"Please let her know that I'll be stopping by tomorrow for my fitting."

"I will, Oma," Inge replied.

Her grandmother, although quite on in years, didn't let that stop her from wanting to be au courant when it came to fashion. The latest trend was to tie a chiffon scarf in a knot about one's neck, and, indeed, Oma had donned an olive green and red one that very evening. With the utmost confidence, Inge recalled that her grandmother was the first in the neighborhood to wear this look.

While Inge did have to share a bed, she couldn't complain about the size of the room. It was large and had some truly modern conveniences such as an attached marble bathroom. There was even a cast-iron radiator rather than a stove that needed to be heated and also a toilet alongside a freestanding tub. Unfortunately for Inge, Grandma Rosa did have some difficulty getting completely used to these modern conveniences. She found it annoying whenever her grandmother needed to urinate during the night because she preferred to use the chamber pot under the bed rather than getting up and going to the toilet.

That night, Inge was so tired that she didn't think about such things. She quickly put on her cotton, rose-printed pajamas, and went straight to bed. Her grandmother joined her soon thereafter. As Inge lay beside her, she waited for the feather-filled quilts to warm up from the heat of their bodies, as she thought about what tomorrow might bring.

In the middle of the night, they were awakened by the constant ringing of their doorbell.

"Who could it be?" she asked herself, half awake, as she raised her head up from the pillow. Quickly, though, she thought the better of it and began falling back to sleep.

"No, I must be dreaming," she thought, as through the slit of her eyes she could tell it was still quite dark outside.

But when the bell kept ringing, she knew that someone had to be at the front door. As she glanced over at the clock sitting on her nightstand, she saw that it was not quite five in the morning. Who might that be coming over at such an hour?

Her grandmother also awoke and promptly got out of bed. Oma made it to the hallway, as Inge's father was already passing by their room, still in his pajamas. He threw on a bathrobe and told them to remain upstairs. Inge could make out the voice of her father's cousin, Isidor, calling out to him.

"Carl, it's me. Open up! Hurry up!"

Her father quickly rushed to open the door, as a frazzled Isidor came stumbling in. He started speaking at top speed about how Nazis were "coming for us, all of us!" Then her father stretched out his hands to steady him, quickly offering him a seat in the parlor.

"Please, Isidor, tell me again," Carl said, "but slowly this time. Exactly what is it that's happening?"

Even after Isidor took a seat, he didn't calm down very much. A slender man with a fair complexion, his face had turned a ghostly white, his hair totally disheveled as though he had been continually wringing his hands through it.

"It's the SA (Hitler's henchmen who formed an unofficial army before he came to power in 1933 but continued to do his dirty work right up till the end of the war in 1945). They are going to all the Jewish homes. And to Jewish businesses. They are smashing them up. Everything! And not only that, they are taking the men away. Pushing them into their cars, removing everybody as though they were criminals!"

Inge, her mother, and grandmother had since moved closer to the landing, near the banister leading downstairs, to better see and hear what was going on. A loud creak escaped from beneath Inge's foot, and her father's cousin looked upward to where they were all standing. His expression was pained, and Inge could tell how he now feared for their safety. Shivers ran up her spine, and thoughts of terror made her heart beat faster. This was the first time she had ever experienced such a primal sense of dread, and as she would later find out, far from the last.

But her father, such a highly respected business owner in the community, believed that his reputation would suffice to exempt them from such treatment and surely from incarceration. If that weren't enough, Carl tried to assure Isidor that, because he had been awarded an Iron Cross by the German government for having served his country so well during the Great War, they didn't have to worry about anything.

He led Isidor upstairs and urged him to lie down and relax in one of the spare rooms. Inge and the other women were instructed by Carl to return to their bedrooms. He told everyone to dress, just in case what would "surely never happen" did take place.

Inge grabbed a pleated red tartan skirt from her closet and paired it with a matching red pullover from a shelf in her armoire. She pulled up her white socks to well above her knees and tied the laces on her sports shoes. She then locked her armoire and placed the key in her pocket, just to be safe.

She sat down to brush her hair in the mirror, parting it to a side, and had the odd thought of how she had always wished she were permitted to wear her hair in two braids with ribbons like other girls. Her mother typically scolded her for such thoughts, saying that it would only serve to have the strength of the child seep down into them, however that could possibly be. Therefore, it was strictly verboten (forbidden).

By then, Oma, too, was also fully dressed. They spent the next two hours in bed waiting for what they hoped would never happen. As the morning light began to brighten the streets of Bremen, Inge allowed herself to relax. They had survived the night without incident, and so they must have been spared for the very reasons her father had stated to Isidor. But just as she felt a bit of release from the tension, there was a loud banging on the front door.

Everyone jumped up and stood at the doorways of their rooms, but this time no one was eager to greet visitors. Her father walked past all of them dressed in his crisp gray suit and diagonally striped tie. His blond hair was slicked neatly back, and he held his chin high and determined. Inge knew her father too well and could tell that behind his unwavering blue eyes, he, too, was fearful.

"Open up!" a voice shouted from the other side of the door.

Vati looked up one last time at Inge, now standing at the top of the stairs. With his eyes, he urged her to stay there as he sighed heavily before opening the door.

The SA men didn't wait for it to be opened completely; they just shoved their way in, the force of these three uninvited and heavily armed men pushing Carl back. She could see that her father seemed to think the better of not taking a belligerent step toward them.

He looked up once more at Inge and the others, as their eyes met momentarily. Carl released his hands from their fisted positions and simply stepped aside to let these low-ranking bullies pass. With a 14-year-old daughter, a wife with a delicate constitution, and his elderly mother-in-law having only him for their protection, he couldn't risk doing anything foolish. It took all of his determination to just stand by and let these men do whatever it was they intended to do.

The three intruders were quite young, but their official Nazi uniforms certainly made them look intimidating. Their brass buttons were polished, as were their high leather boots, as they tramped their way into the dining room. After barely looking about, they took the swords from their hilts and sent them crashing down on all of Oma's fine china.

From where they were situated, neither Inge, her mother, grandmother, nor Isidor could tell exactly what was happening. All they could hear was the glass smashing, but it was enough to make Grandma Rosa waver at the damage being inflicted in her home. She grasped Inge's hand and grabbed at her chest with the other. Inge and her mother Marianne immediately took her by her arms and led Oma back to her bed. Mutti gently laid her down on some pillows, as Inge raised her feet. Grandma Rosa began breathing heavily and had grown quite pale, but Inge felt that if she could manage to relax her that she would be all right. The stress of what was happening was undoubtedly putting tremendous strain on her already existing heart condition.

Inge took one of Oma's pills from her bedside table and filled a glass with water from the bathroom. Oma appeared to respond, and her heavy breathing soon began to slow. With Marianne now in enough control of herself to manage her mother's condition, Inge went back to the landing to see what was happening. She made out many tiny white specs all over the red carpeting, which ran down the hallway between the dining and living rooms, as well as throughout the rest of the first floor of the house.

"Oh my," she thought at first, *"it must be snowing already in November."*

As the crashing of glass continued, one of the SA men pulled her father aside for questioning. How many were residing in the house, he demanded to know, what their names were, ages, etc. After her father answered each inquiry truthfully, the man went into the kitchen where Inge could see him pick up the phone.

"Yes. Four of them...we'll need the car sent over...four, yes... hello? Sir, can you hear me? Hello?"

Her father calmly and politely as possible approached the young man. He did not know him because the Nazis had selected men who weren't from Bremen to vandalize the Jewish homes there and imprison its occupants.

"We will wait here," her father promised solemnly. "Go fetch your car. We'll be here when you return."

Carl looked the officers straight in the eyes as he said this, and, after considering it for a moment, the young man, somewhat surprisingly, agreed. He called to the others and told them what was going to take place. They put their swords back in place, and all left through the front door.

Inge ran down the stairway to meet her father and to see what had transpired. She rushed into his awaiting arms—but whether it was for her own comfort or his, she wasn't sure. She could feel the bumps on the carpeting beneath her feet. No, it was not snow that lined the floor, as she had initially thought. Rather, they were little bits of the dinner dishes she had cleaned that evening and put away. These pieces must have loosened after having gotten stuck between the ridges of the soldiers' boots, as they vandalized their way through the rooms.

Why had her life changed so much in just a few short hours? Last night her home was still an untouched refuge from the ever-looming threats of the Nazis. The walls had remained a bastion protecting them from the terrors growing throughout Germany. Laughing and eating over good food with her family seated around the dining table, they could momentarily forget about what was happening outside. But now that very same dining room was barely recognizable. Her father held her by the shoulders in fear that she may cut herself on something sharp.

No longer would she ever again hear the chiming of the grandfather clock. The long white Shabbat candles in their sterling silver holders had been hurled through its glass face, and the front cabinet door, now ripped off, exposed gears that were bent and broken, and another candlestick had impaled its chains. As she looked away, almost as if to avoid being a voyeur at a crime scene, she only confronted more horrors. Framed family pictures that once hung on the walls or stood on the tops of cabinets had been defiled. The faces of each member, even babies, had been slashed by the soldier's swords.

Inge stood frozen by the shock at the unimaginable and reckless destruction. Only a shrill cry from Mutti tore her away from this trance-like state. She and her father immediately ran over to where her mother was then standing at the bottom of the staircase. Both insisted that she shouldn't look around, but Marianne wouldn't listen. She walked through each room with one hand covering her mouth, carefully stepping over the broken lamps that had been tossed to the floor and the smashed porcelain vases that had once held roses cut from bushes in the yard. It wasn't until Inge's mother made her way to the "Wintergarten" that she was totally overcome with grief.

It was her beloved room, a greenhouse of sorts, one filled to capacity with potted plants—everything from begonias to violets to rubber plants. During the long, cold, German winter months, this room had served as an eternal springtime for Mutti. Every day during that time of year, she would spend long hours on that floral outdoor furniture just sipping tea and reading her books. It was such a warm and inviting space. Seeing all the broken pots on the floor and her plants trampled, it was too much for Marianne to take. She began to grow faint. Inge and her father then each took Marianne by an arm and quickly led her upstairs, placing Marianne on the bed beside her mother. She was given a glass of water, and Carl placed a damp rag on her head. Inge's father then explained everything that had taken place.

"They are coming back for us. All of us," he said. "I do not know what they want, or what they will do. We can only pray that whatever happens, they will allow us all to stay together."

Inge could feel her hands grow cold and asked why they shouldn't try to escape while these men were away. There must be somewhere safe they could run off to. But her father was adamant; he had given the Nazis his word. Inge and the others would never dare to further challenge Carl's authority. They all remained in that room together as they waited for the Nazis to return.

Shortly after that, the front door swung noisily open. To their relief, they heard cousin Ruthie's familiar voice shouting up to them.

"*Onkel* Carl! *Onkel* Carl!"

Still out of breath, with her overcoat unbuttoned and her hair tousled by the wind, it seemed she had run the three streets separating their homes as fast as she could. Carl immediately questioned her regarding the safety of her parents.

"My mother, sister, and I were hiding under a bed when these men began rampaging through our home. I came to warn you."

She began to take notice of all the wreckage and stopped mid-sentence.

"Oh, how awful! I see that I have come too late."

As Ruthie spoke those words and feeling as despondently as the rest, she straightened her wire-rimmed glasses and said to her Uncle Carl, "But don't worry, my father was upstairs when they shot open our door. He managed to jump out a window, hopped over the fence to our yard, and went directly to the police station. Don't be concerned any more, help will be arriving shortly."

Hearing her naiveté, Carl held onto his niece's shoulders even more firmly. With a mix of sadness and unquestioning authority, he told his young niece to return home to where she might avoid the harm they will shortly be subjected to.

"The troopers are coming back for us in a few moments," he stated. "You are not safe here. You must leave."

Ruthie failed to comprehend what he was saying. She looked at him with questioning eyes, but Inge's father only repeated the same thing, only more emphatically this time. "Go. Go now. Before it's too late!"

Inge's family didn't have to wait much longer, only about half an hour, before the German officers returned. This time they came in without bothering to knock.

"We only need the men," one said authoritatively.

Upon hearing this, Inge thought of her father's business partner who'd been sent to Poland with his daughter several months earlier and was never heard from again. She rushed to Vati's room and retrieved a pair of his woolen socks and a handkerchief. She had heard Poland could become quite cold and thought these would serve him well were his nose to run.

Her father was already following the Nazis out the door when Inge rushed down the stairs to give him these items. As she shoved everything into a pocket of his coat, with equal parts fear and resolve in his heart, he momentarily drew her close for what was perhaps one last time.

"Take your mother and grandmother to the taxi stand and go to Frau Beiser's home," he said to her in a hushed voice while his cheek was still pressed against her hair.

As Carl let go of his daughter and walked down the path of their home, he drew a modicum of comfort in knowing that at least for now the women were safe. But when—if ever—would he be able to return to protect them? As he was being led away, Inge prayed that this would not be the last time she would set her eyes upon her father.

Carl Katz, 18, in his military uniform. During the Great War, WWI. Having served on the front lines during that conflict, he was awarded a medal.

Chapter Two

Shards of Glass

Inge, 14, posing with her mother Marianne in 1938.

Inge lingered outside her home even after the vehicle carrying her father disappeared down the road. The street was now surprisingly quiet given the devastation. Most everyone witnessing what occurred had to be in shock, even immobilized, but Inge, only 14, withstood its horrors better than most. There wasn't time for her to be overwhelmed or dismayed. Paralyzing fear was a luxury she refused to indulge in. Quickly, she stepped back inside away from the crisp chill of November air, closing the heavy front door behind her.

Unlike the others in her family, she sensed how important it was for all of them to get away from there before it was too late. She practically flew back upstairs to impress upon her mother and grandmother to get ready. Their home was no longer a safe place to be. Perhaps more troopers were already on their way, this time to gather up women and children. As she rushed into her grandmother's bedroom, where she also slept, Isidor, whom the Germans hadn't seized, was doing what he could to calm the two women. Possibly the Nazis both allowed him to stay because he claimed that he was just visiting from out of town.

Inge related what her father told her they must do. "We must take a taxi and go straight to Frau Beiser. I'll get your coats, and let's get out of here right away." Inge practically ordered them.

To save time while the women readied themselves, Inge gathered their belongings. Even at such a pressing moment, she did her best to coordinate the clothes they would be taking with matching pairs of shoes. Once packed, she unfastened the gold clasps on all of their respective snake - skinned purses to stuff into other smaller necessities: crocheted handkerchiefs, a few Reichsmark, and some Baldrian, a sedative mixed into sugar cubes. All four of them went downstairs, with Inge leading the way.

As they reached the ground floor, Inge turned to her grandmother, saying, "Oma, take my arm, and be careful where you walk." With so much breakage around, one can't be too careful. Inge wanted them to remain as steadfast as possible. This was no time for complications. They walked as they usually did toward the taxi stand, but nothing felt the same that morning. Many of the people walking past them, they knew, were on their way to work. Inge found herself feeling resentful, even suspicious of them. *Didn't they realize what was happening but were doing nothing? How could they act like that?* Yet no one, as they hurried by, even took any notice of them. No one inquired as to whether they were all right or about Carl's whereabouts. They had become like strangers; these Germans remained silent even after having witnessed the suffering of their Jewish neighbors. Inge thought how odd this was. Everyone acted as if nothing different had happened since yesterday, while for Inge and her family, nothing was the same.

The taxi stand was situated right at the corner of the street where her cousin Ruthie and her family lived. As the three of them reached her tree-lined street, their regular taxi driver was there. He assisted them with their belongings. He seemed like the only neighbor to express any concern for them.

"Frau Gruenberg! Frau Gruenberg!" he called breathlessly. "Your daughter. A terrible thing has happened to her!"

Grandma Rosa's other daughter, Frieda, and Inge's mother, were sisters. Ruthie, Inge's cousin, was Frieda's daughter.

"Yes, I heard," Oma replied. "We must go by their home and pick them up."

Inge didn't say a word but felt as if her heart had suddenly stopped. *What if they had already been taken? Might they have been harmed?* After all, Ruthie was her closest friend.

When she saw Ruthie, along with her sister Mary, and Tante Frieda, after Mutti had knocked on their door, Inge was practically ecstatic. After tear-filled hugs and an emotional exchange of words, they all followed Grandma Rosa into the taxi to set off for Frau Beiser's. Ruthie managed to sit next to Inge, so they, too, like their elders, could talk to one another more readily. Beneath her tan wool overcoat, Inge could see that Ruthie was wearing her Norwegian-style cardigan with the pretty white and red flowers embroidered over the navy-blue wool. *How good it looked on her,* Inge thought. In spite of all that transpired, she found herself feeling disappointed that she had not coordinated the sweater she had worn that morning with Ruthie's. Inge and Ruthie always had a penchant for wearing matching outfits. One would rarely go shopping at Heymann and Neumann's Department Store without the other.

As the taxi drove them to Frau Beiser's home in the center of Bremen, a twenty-minute ride, its occupants became increasingly tense and silent. They were heading to the home of Carl's business partner, Max Beiser. He, with his daughter, had been forced to leave Germany six months earlier for Poland, where he was born. But Frau Beiser, his German wife, who was not Jewish, was allowed to remain. Because Carl thought so highly of his partner's wife, and sure that she would care for them, he reasoned that his family would be safer staying at her home.

Just as they pulled up in front of the tiled steps of the Beiser's stately townhouse and had barely exited the cab, the front door with its heavy brass knocker swung open, and Frau Beiser appeared, ready to greet them. Tall and slender, with her blonde hair neatly pulled back, and a string of pearls around her neck poking through the collar of her white silk blouse, she grasped each one in turn as she greeted them, all the while expressing tremendous relief with her eyes.

"Thank goodness," she repeated several times as she quickly ushered them all inside. "I've been worried sick about all of you! Please hand me your coats, and then go join the others."

Each did as requested once they crossed over the threshold. In the center of the foyer sat a carved wooden table with a large crystal vase on top of it filled with white and yellow chrysanthemums. Inge made a concerted effort not to bump into it as she took off her coat.

"What did Frau Besier mean when she said 'the others,'?" Inge wondered—and as soon as she entered the grand parlor, she saw that it was filled practically to capacity with other Jews also trying to avoid the Nazis: men, women, and children, all most anxious. They had come because, like her father, they felt they would be safer there.

All those sitting upon the sofas and chairs in that room were relatives of Herr Beiser. They were drinking coffee and had plates filled with bread, fruit, and cookies on their laps. All were dressed rather casually and holding polite conversations with one another. Had it not been for the desperation she could sense in their eyes, she might have thought a party was going on.

This home was furnished throughout with polished wood flooring and numerous rugs. Heavy velvet drapery in varying hues of forest green framed the perimeters of enormous floor-length windows facing the street. Inge and Ruthie found an unoccupied dining room chair on which they managed to sit together next to one of those windows and could observe the passersby.

Between mouthfuls of bread and jam, they spoke in low voices about all that had happened last night. Being with Ruthie, Inge could express her true feelings and not have to pretend to be brave and strong. It was Ruthie, actually, who was always the braver and protected Inge. Inge's nature was much more reserved, and she was always grateful to have such an outspoken and confident companion by her side. She confided to Ruthie her deepest fears, asking one question right after another: "Where do you think they have taken the men? What will they be doing to them? When will they be coming home? What if, G-d forbid, they have also been taken to Poland like Herr Beiser? Will we ever see them again?"

Inge then got up to gather some cookies on her white china plate and refill her teacup, after which the girls continued voicing their concerns to one another. They had become so involved that they barely heard the knock upon the door or even noticed when Frau Beiser went to open it. Everyone's conversations ceased as a woman in an official-looking tan suit came into the room. She might have gone unnoticed by all were it not for the large swastika fastened to her lapel.

She was tall and rather heavy-set, with her shoulder-length blonde hair neatly pulled back tightly in a bun. Otherwise, her features were rather plain and coarse. She would never have been considered pretty. She appeared contemplative as she took notice of all those present. Inge recognized her immediately. It was Frau Beiser's sister.

Inge and her family had always been treated by her with kindness and respect, even though they had always known she was an active member of the Frauenschaft, the women's group associated with the Nazi party. Before the previous night, rather than fearing Frau Beiser's sister's affiliation, they believed that women like her might be able to influence the Nazi party to go in a better direction. Now Inge was not so sure. She could no longer trust her and wondered why she was showing up there that morning. Inge was ready to believe that she was there to find out who was hiding in her sister's home and to report them to the authorities.

Everyone in the room focused on her in anticipation. Inge had always known this woman to be close to her niece, Frau Beiser's daughter, then in Poland, and fond of all of her brother-in-law's family. She gave each person in the room a warm greeting. Smiles soon appeared on their apprehensive faces. Inge, like the others, was relieved that Frau Beiser's sister had not become like her family's neighbors who were avoiding the Jews.

Still, an overwhelming heaviness of heart remained within Inge. Perhaps they were being too hasty in trusting her. From her chair near the window, she could see two uniformed SA officers making their way up the steps to the house. Frau Beiser's sister began to quietly warn the others, but Inge shouted out, "They are coming for us now. You must run and hide!" Hopefully there was enough time for everyone to escape as the men all scrambled to their feet. Frau Beiser urged them to run quickly out the back door and hide in the warehouse.

The rest, the ten women and children, had no choice but to remain where they were. One and all tried to appear calm. Inge rushed to her mother and grandmother, seated herself between them, and held out her hands to each.

Just as everyone's anxiety was reaching new heights, Frau Beiser's sister announced, "Please, remain calm. I'll take care of this," and went out of the parlor.

Although Inge and the others wanted to trust her, they couldn't help but wonder how was it that these SA men had shown up so soon after the sister's arrival. Inge held on to her mother and grandmother's hands a bit tighter to keep them from shaking. Her remaining faith in the goodness of the German people was fast disappearing, but she had no choice but to trust this woman. As she heard her answer the door, Inge held her breath and did her best to listen.

"Heil Hitler!" She audibly greeted the officers. "Heil Hitler!" the men replied in kind.

As much as Inge strained to listen, she could only make out a few words. The conversation lasted but a minute before they all heard the front door close with a bang. Heavy footsteps resounding off of the wooden floor could be heard as the sister reentered, and Marianne raised her free hand to place over her mouth in anticipation. But the only one there was Frau Beiser's sister. The others had gone.

"I told them that this was an Aryan household," she reported. "They won't return."

There was a sigh of audible relief as the women and children regained their composure and began to move about. It appeared that each was getting ready to approach her. Truly, here was a woman who had just risked her own well-being to protect theirs. Each attempted to express their appreciation, but she wouldn't hear of it.

"Please, just don't mention it," was all she answered.

After a while, the sister left this cluster of frightened and vulnerable family members and friends to return to her own home. That morning was the last time Inge ever saw or heard from her. She often wondered whether the Nazis had ever discovered that the sister had saved them that morning. And if so, if she was ever punished for it.

Given the disconcerting events of that morning, all of Herr Beiser's family members decided not to remain there. It was now painfully evident to all that Germany was no longer tolerable for Jews. There was no hope that another political party might come to power or that they would be able to endure the increasingly discriminatory laws. Their only recourse was to pick up the shattered pieces of their lives and to do whatever they could to get out of Germany. Most of them spent the rest of that day trying to figure out how best to flee the country. However, that would prove increasingly impossible. Had they decided to do so a couple of months earlier, it would have been more feasible.

Frau Beiser would not think of having Inge and her family leave her home that day. She had grown close to all of them over the years and knew what delicate constitutions Marianne and her mother had. Moreover, they were the only ones thus far who had the man in their family taken away by the Nazis. She kept feeding them throughout that day and gave them all warm beds for the night. Inge and Ruthie wanted to sleep together in her daughter Etty's room.

That night, Inge could not help but feel like a princess, being in such a grand bedroom. The furniture was painted brilliant white, and the linens were of the most beautiful crocheted blankets, lace trimmed sheets, and down comforters. Frau Beiser loved to dote on her only child and would spend countless hours sewing and crocheting all her daughter's clothes. She was quite a gifted seamstress, and Inge was always amazed by her craftsmanship. It was because of a party where Etty walked in wearing a gorgeous yellow party dress that Inge decided that she, too, wanted to become a dressmaker. As Inge settled under the covers that night, she felt a twinge of sadness come over her. She hoped that one day soon Frau Beiser would be reunited with Etty and prayed that she was still safe.

In spite of how comfortable that bed was, Inge didn't sleep well at all. Her sleep was broken by nightmares about what might be happening to her father. Images of him lying on a dirty jail cell floor or being made to walk through heavy snow in some desolate place kept waking her. One of her dreams even imagined him starving and bent over a garbage can as all his hair was being shaved off. Each time she awoke, she uttered a prayer for his safety and that he would be returning to them shortly.

After a brief breakfast the next morning, everyone headed back to their respective homes, although Inge had no desire to return. Her mother and grandmother insisted, though. They wanted to try establishing life as it was before, even though they were not entirely sure it would be possible. For Inge, that house from then on would serve only as a reminder of that awful day when her sanctuary from the outside world had been violated.

Her home at 33 Isarstrasse would forever after serve only as a reminder of the haphazard and reckless destruction of her life and the foreshadowing of all that was still to come. It was then that the actual Jewish "situation" throughout Germany became most real to the adolescent Inge. Unaware at the time, of course, of what was to come, but just by returning to witness the physical and emotional damage, she began to reevaluate not only her own life but the lives of those around her. As she tossed the shards of glass on the floor of the Wintergarten into garbage cans, she realized that nothing ever would be the same again for her and her family.

All three women worked tirelessly for the next several days trying to rid their home of the desecration those SA brutes had wrought. They set things back in their proper places, took down the ruined pictures, removing them from their frames, and returned the Shabbat candlesticks to their rightful place on the mantel. They wondered how it would be to celebrate the Sabbath that coming Friday evening without Carl. Several days had passed, and still no word regarding his whereabouts. It seemed as if he were still around, having been such a dominating presence, one who governed every aspect of their lives.

Inge often had to remind herself not to set a place for him at the table and not to stare at his favorite armchair in the evenings where he always rested after a long day at the office. The crystal ashtray remained on the side table next to his chair, as if it, too, were suspended in time, just waiting for his return.

Inge and her mother continued to dress up every day so as to appear at their best were Carl to suddenly swing open the front door as he always did, with a warm smile beaming, and his arms open to receive them. But each new day followed the last without him.

About a week after the night that came to be known as "Kristallnacht," there was word that some of the men had returned. Inge's mother did her hair and carefully applied her makeup, ready to greet her husband at the train station. Every evening after dinner, she would go to the platform, hoping to greet him as he stepped off one of the incoming trains—and every night she would return home alone to an expectant Inge waiting at the foot of the stairwell. With her head hanging down, Marianne would quietly say, "Tomorrow, Inge. Tomorrow, for sure, he will be back." She would then smile half-heartedly at Inge before going back upstairs to retire for the night.

Days came and went with no news, and soon three weeks had passed. Inge tried not to give up hope, but she began to fear that he wouldn't ever return. Maybe she had to accept this new reality and begin learning how to live life without her father. But one evening when her mother came back after waiting at the train platform, Inge was surprised to see her smiling. It was then that she saw the silhouette of a man standing behind Marianne in the doorway, and she momentarily grew expectant before she felt her heart again sink.

Yes, there was a man there with Mutti, but he did not look like her father. The person who entered their foyer looked so much older and very tired. He was bald and far thinner than she had ever known. The father she knew was always impeccably dressed. He would never have allowed himself to be seen in such a rumpled, dirty, and ill-fitting suit. But once he stepped further into the light, she caught sight of his familiar blue eyes. His shoulders, now weighed down from unknowable burdens, straightened somewhat upon sight of her, and he opened his arms to embrace his daughter.

Carl being home restored Inge's hope that something positive might now be in store for the family. Inge knew that Vati would make sure she would be all right.

Chapter Three

Deportation

Inge, 15, at a picnic during her stay with Tante Berta in Berlin in 1939.

It was much easier said than done for Carl to make everything right again for his family as well as for himself. As Kristallnacht portended, Jews were not only unwelcome in Germany, but now they were no longer even tolerated. A mad rush arose within the Jewish community to get out of Germany by whatever means possible. Some c o n t a c t e d relatives abroad, others visited the consulate offices of countries as far away as South America and Australia. There were even those who closed their businesses in the belief that they would be able to leave.

Herr Beiser, Frau Beiser's husband, was temporarily permitted to re-enter Germany from Poland in order to liquidate all of his assets, including the company he owned jointly with Inge's father. Without his business to keep him occupied, and since the leader of the Bremen Jewish community, renamed the Reichsvertretung der Juden in Deutschland Bremen by the Nazis, having fled to the United States, Carl then willingly accepted the position of second in command. Along with many Jewish-owned businesses and homes, the local synagogue had been destroyed during Kristallnacht, the structure having burned completely to the ground. Communal meetings and all prayer services since then were being held in the home of Inge's mother's cousin, Alfred Gruenberg.

His home, in fact, became Bremen's official Jewish Community Center, with a different operation held on each floor. Carl devoted most of his time to caring for the elderly. He also knew the vice consulate of Ecuador very well and worked tirelessly with him to arrange for safe passage for his extended family to that country. He took his responsibility as community leader quite seriously and therefore refused to leave Germany with Inge, Marianne, and her mother while there was still so much he could still do for others.

Had he realized that this period within which to escape would be so brief, surely he would have done things differently. In spite of his having made tentative arrangements for his immediate family to leave, it was not to be. Indeed, on the very day that the family expected to collect their visas, Jews were no longer allowed to do so. Their fate had been sealed.

None of them said much about what this restriction bode for them. Actually, they didn't know at that time. As they returned home after being unable to obtain their visas, they all felt dejected. Passing all their non-Jewish neighbors, continuing to go about their daily activities, the Nazis had put them into an impossible position. True, while most countries were refusing to accept them in any numbers, Germany neither wanted them to remain nor to leave, even if they could arrange to do so. Now there was nowhere for Jews to run. No sanctuary. Inge began to feel vulnerable right there in Bremen, her childhood home where she had always felt so safe. What was she to do now? Just wait for more injustices to befall? She couldn't allow herself to dwell upon her current situation and wile away the hours of each day doing nothing. She needed to feel useful and productive and to keep herself occupied so she wouldn't constantly be thinking about their dire situation. But how?

Inge decided that she and Ruthie must figure out some other means of employment because Frau Herzberg, their now former employer, had been able to leave for America shortly after her husband had been arrested on Kristallnacht but then released from one of the camps afterward. It also bothered Inge that Ruthie and her family, too, were unable to get out of Germany when Jews were still able to leave, although neither could she imagine life without being with her dearest companion. Perhaps the two of them might still be able to figure out some way to continue taking sewing classes in pursuit of their dream to open their own Atelier someday.

Several weeks later, something unfortunate happened, the passing of Inge's paternal grandfather, Opa Rudolph, but which, however, presented an opportunity for Inge. Her aunt and uncle had come from Berlin to attend the funeral. Tante Berta, Carl's sister, wanted to care for her mother, the now widowed Oma Pauline, by having her go back to her home in Berlin to live there with her. Just a few days later, Inge, along with her parents, boarded a train for Berlin to help Carl's mother with the move.

Tante Berta was particularly thankful to have Inge with her in her home at that time. It had seemed so long since she had had her own two young daughters to fill the halls with life and laughter. They had been sent off for their safety to a "foreign land," to Palestine. One, to stay with family members, and the other, to live on a kibbutz. But by doing so, Tante Berta was haunted every waking moment, wondering whether her children were safe and being well-cared for. Still, she knew deep down that it was far better for them there than in Germany.

Inge, who remained in Berlin at her aunt's request, with her parents' approval, became a comfort and joy to her aunt. After all, because Berlin was far larger than Bremen, Tante Berta immediately sought out possible opportunities for Inge there in the hope that her niece would be willing to remain. Knowing how close Inge was to her parents, she knew it would not be an easy choice for her to make. And so, the next morning right after they arrived, Tante Berta took Inge to the Jewish Community Center where women were being taught useful trades. She could have arranged for Inge to be enrolled in a candy-making course, or making artificial flowers, or one for beauticians, but none of those appealed to Inge. What she really wanted was to continue her studies to become a seamstress. When they passed a room filled with young girls her own age, all of whom were sewing, Inge became excited and wanted to enroll in that class.

After spending time convincing and assuring her parents that she would not be a burden to her aunt, surprisingly, she thought, her parents agreed to allow her to stay. They were astonished that Inge was not afraid to be away from home for the two-year-long certification program. Although she would surely miss her parents and especially Ruthie, she figured they could remain in touch by phone. Besides, it was just a half-a- day's train ride away.

Carl and Marianne, with some reluctance, decided to allow Inge to remain in Berlin. Above all, they wanted her to be happy; they felt that the change would take her away from a setting that had become so traumatic for her. Inge, too, wondered, whether that was the real reason she was so eager to make the change.

Although Inge hoped that she would finally be getting a room of her own at Tante Berta's, she found herself once again sharing one. This time it would be with her other grandmother, another grieving widow. Oma Pauline, though, had always been kind to her and used to make the most delicious Butterkuchen (a German cake). But that was long ago. Now she was suffering from dementia, and Inge would often awaken to find her standing in front of a mirror and speaking to her own reflection. Rarely did she comprehend that her husband was gone and would often spend whole evenings looking out the window in anticipation of his returning home from the office.

Inge didn't mind her grandmother's behavior all that much. She was happy because it was so good being with the girls in the sewing program who had turned out to be so welcoming and nice. Soon enough, they were all great friends, back in school once again. This time she was not an outsider. She felt now that she truly belonged. And so it was, in this small classroom, where she would spend her days from early morning until late afternoon that she learned how to make patterns and sew clothing.

Pattern samples Inge and the other girls from her class would construct.

Initially, her stay in Berlin was intended to be brief, just to help settle Oma Pauline, and so Inge arrived with but a few changes of clothing. Learning her trade, however, turned out to be a great opportunity for her to craft the beautiful fabrics her mother would send into stylish blouses, skirts, and jackets for herself.

Inge was genuinely coming to enjoy her new life in such a cosmopolitan city. Everything for the time being felt surprisingly normal and comfortable as she became increasingly at home in Berlin. Even when, after being there for nearly six months, there was an announcement on the radio that World War II had begun, it barely affected her. It was September 1939, and while she understood that this was a serious time for everyone, it actually meant very little to a 15-year-old like herself. Moreover, it didn't seem real. Rarely did she see airplanes flying overhead or hear soldiers marching through the streets. There was nothing like that.

It took nearly a half year following its outbreak that the local newspapers began to report the bombing of cities. Then Inge started to become increasingly anxious about what might happen were the Allied troops to bomb Berlin or Bremen. The war would then no longer be something distant, something happening elsewhere. One morning in particular, while she was in sewing class, she suddenly found herself worried about her family's safety. She felt as if she were too far away from them. And, as if she'd had a premonition, when she returned home from her class that evening, she received an urgent call from her father. "Inge, it is time for you to come home," was all he said to her in his deep and authoritative voice.

She somewhat begrudgingly packed her belongings as her father had instructed and bade farewell to all her classmates as well as her aunt and uncle. It was not that she was reluctant about being back with her parents, not at all. She never wanted to stop being together with them, especially if, G-d forbid, anything were to happen. It was just that, for one fleeting year, she felt like she was just a normal girl, leading a happy life, and well on her way to achieving her dream of opening up her own Atelier with Ruthie. In Berlin, she had felt so far away from reality, which is how Germany was planning to handle its "Jewish problem."

Upon returning to Bremen, Inge didn't return to 33 Isarstrasse to live. Rather, her parents had been ordered to move to Legion-Condor-Strasse 1, to what had become known as Das Judenhaus (The Jewish House). This way, the Nazis decided, it would be easier for them to keep track of the Jews, that is, keeping them all in more concentrated locations. Inge's family was housed on the first floor of a house that had once belonged to a cousin of Adolf Gruenberg (husband of Grandma

Rosa). Days of comfortable and proper living were now gone. The three of them had to share just two rooms, one became their living room, and the other their bedroom, which had but one single bed. Inge had no option but to sleep on a chaise lounge at one end of her parents' bed. Just across the hall from them was the Frank family: the husband, wife, their three sons, and the wife's brother. At the far end of the floor was a single room where Frau Aronstein lived by herself. They all had to use a single bathroom.

In the basement was the kitchen, which everyone shared, and next to it a small room where two elderly gentlemen, Herr Frank, and Herr Fogel, stayed. It seemed to Inge they were always down there peeling potatoes. The kitchen was certainly not fancy, but it did serve its purpose. There were two stoves, a large sink, and plenty of standing cabinets for plates and other serving ware. In the center of the room, tiled in black and white, was a large rectangular table where everyone ate.

Inge liked the Franks for the most part, but she often felt uncomfortable when heated arguments erupted between Frau Frank and Frau Aronstein. It wasn't easy for these two domineering women to share a single kitchen. The adjustment both had to make from the life of luxury to the life of poverty brought out the worst in them. The tension was frequently high.

On the other two floors in the house there were separate kitchens, so thankfully, those residents didn't add to the chaos when meals had to be prepared. On the second floor were the Jonas and Horowitz families, along with a second Horowitz family that had settled in with a niece. The third floor was occupied by the Hertz family, Frau Wortheimer and her two children, and a Jewish woman with her non-Jewish husband, Herr J. Lisiak. The Nazis had put this man in charge to monitor all the others and to report anything of note back to them. Inge, like everyone else, neither liked nor trusted this man.

He would always, most suspiciously, need to work on the furnace in the kitchen during their mealtimes. As it turned out, Inge's family would often receive special offerings from shopkeepers. It appeared to Inge that they did so because it upset them to see children denied the healthy food they needed. They would secretly add such items into Inge's packages that she would then share with all the other families. Some of these merchants even left groceries for them on the doorstep. The man from the local fish store would also purposely place shopping bags in front of his door when he knew that any of the Katzes would be passing by on their way back from the synagogue. They would then have to take great care to conceal such additional foods that Jews were not permitted to purchase from Herr J. Lisiak.

Among the various tenants residing in the Judenhaus, Inge found that the most interesting one lived on the top floor. One could usually find her shuffling to and fro, with her frail body bent forward under the weight of the large hump protruding from her back. She would always have a deck of cards with her and told everyone to call her Tante Marta. Inge didn't believe that that was really her name, but she liked her, and she even allowed her once to tell her a fortune using that deck of cards. "Aah..." she sighed mystically, as she laid out the cards before her. "A very good fortune, indeed," she said, smiling kindly at Inge. "Plenty of money, and lots of love from a good family, and a good man, I see..."

Inge was not so sure that she believed in fortune telling, but those particular words never left her. She would even find herself repeating them in her head whenever she was alone during the terrible times that followed.

Even though life had changed so dramatically for all of them, Inge and her family still felt there was no reason to allow it to disrupt their day-to-day activities. There was always work to be done and chores to be completed. While the government now prevented Inge from continuing with any formal education, she was determined not to let that deter her from achieving her goals.

Shortly thereafter, she and Ruthie began to search for their next employment opportunity, and soon enough they did come upon one. It was a far cry from the stately residence of Frau Herzberg's Atelier. It was not an upscale townhouse in the center of the fashion district, just a small one bedroom apartment on the ground floor of a three-story walk-up. There was no work area set aside where the customers could be attended to, and there was merely a plain simple wooden board thrown over the bed that served as a workstation for cutting patterns.

The dressmaker, Frau Goldschmidt, aside from her tough demeanor, was nice enough, Inge thought. The last several years had been hard on this woman. She was originally from the small town of Delmenhorst, but when the Nazis forced all the Jews there to move into larger communities, she had to come to Bremen. It was a difficult transition for her. She was not used to cramped living quarters, with such street noise. Frau Goldschmidt longed for her former life with more pastoral meadows and open spaces. She missed her neighbors and the relatives she had spent the better part of a lifetime with. Most of all, she longed for her children.

Desperate and frightened, she arranged for her two young children to be sent to Great Britain on one of the rescue missions, called the Kindertransport, which took place during the nine months prior to the outbreak of the Second World War. They were staying with foster families, but the uncertainty regarding their well-being, and whether she would ever see them again, weighed heavily upon her.

As Inge and Ruthie sat before her demonstrating their sewing abilities, Frau Goldschmidt lowered her glasses and looked at each of the two girls critically. She was looking to hire just one girl to help her with alterations. "You," she remarked to Ruthie, through her thin lips pressed together in disapproval. "You can attend my course," something she also offered as part of her business. "And you," she continued curtly as she rested her small brown eyes on Inge. "You can start working here tomorrow, first thing. Don't be late."

Frau Goldschmidt then straightened her work apron about her waist, pushed a stray strand of brown hair from her brow, and sat down behind a sewing machine to continue working on a garment. The two girls looked at one another, and Ruthie just shrugged. This would have to do.

"I thought your French seam was perfect," Inge said to Ruthie after they had stepped out from the stone entryway and were away from the building.

"Thanks," Ruthie said and added with a smile, "but we both know you're a great seamstress. You deserve to have this job. Congratulations."

Inge and Ruthie were together once more as they had been almost two years earlier. "Could it have been that long already?" Inge thought to herself. The year was now 1940, and Inge had reached the age of 16. Already two years had passed since Kristallnacht. Living in that large house with her mother, father, and grandmother, where she had spent her time (after completing her chores, of course) playing hopscotch and jump rope with Ruthie and the other neighborhood children.

When she thought about those days, the sky, trees, and flowers in her memory appeared quite different than those around her now. Even though she was still living in the same part of Bremen, the sky never appeared to be as clear or as blue as it did in her memories of 33 Isarstrasse. Her recollections of playing in the front yard and on the street facing their home depicted her and the other children playing in crisp white or yellow linens. Now she sensed that everyone, including herself, were dressing in hues of navy, taupe, and gray. When she walked along the path to school or town, she remembered them as being tree-lined and covered with rose bushes, and there were flower boxes on the window ledges overflowing with begonias. But now all she saw were the thick cobblestones she stepped upon with caution, so as to avoid turning an ankle.

In spite of it all, Inge remained a fighter at heart and knew that, whatever she might be confronted with, she would still always find something positive, even in the worst of situations. After all, how lucky she was to again be able to work alongside of Ruthie. She had missed her so terribly that year she had been living in Berlin. Inge now wished that she could have invited Ruthie to be with her, if only her parents would have allowed it.

But that no longer mattered; after all, they were now together. The year they spent in that tiny room of Frau Goldschmidt's dress shop, they managed to really enjoy themselves.

Sometimes Frau Goldschmidt would permit them to use scrap pieces of fabric and fur for their own creations, and they had great fun making themselves matching outfits and accessories. One of their favorite creations was a navy-blue pillbox hat, with a strip of mink fur along the front. They thought they looked so divine. In fact, they even arranged to have a photo taken with them on. They had a sneaking suspicion, though, that one day they would look upon that picture and feel quite foolish at how serious and proud they were in such a get up. But certainly not today. They were going to walk about with their heads held high because Ruthie wanted to make sure that everyone would see just how fabulous and talented the two of them were.

However, it wasn't long before the uncertainty she had been running away from no longer permitted her any illusions of normalcy. The latest instance of it was the Nazi decree that all Jews over the age of six must have a Gelben Stern, a cloth patch depicting the six-pointed, yellow Star of David sewn onto their clothing, with the word "JUDE" (Jew) appearing on it. After the initial shock, Inge, once more, regained her footing, along with her usual positive and can-do attitude. She decided it really didn't bother her all that much to wear the star.

While the Germans meant it to be a mark of shame and ostracism, Inge felt quite proud to have it adorn the side of her jackets on top of her heart. After all, wasn't she a Jew? Not only had she always been proud of her heritage, she never even wished, much less pretended, to be anyone other than who she was. Besides, everyone within the community already knew who the Jews were, so she felt this way of identifying them to merely be a silly overstatement of the obvious.

When she walked through the streets of Bremen or stood in the back of the trams, as Jews were no longer permitted either to sit or to be in the front, surprisingly, no one ever treated her with hostility or made her feel as if she were being isolated. In fact, she thought, that it made many of the non-Jews regard her with some compassion. When food was rationed for the Jews, there were even some shop owners who threw in something extra, sometimes even food Jews were forbidden to purchase. She couldn't tell whether this was the case for everyone who wore the star, but it was what she experienced for the next several months.

Even with all this, Inge thought, it was an existence she felt she could get used to. They had all, in fact, become quite adept at making the best of difficult situations. For example, rather than feeling overwhelmed by the number of people living in a single house, these young ones, along with others their age, used it as an opportunity to hold dances, which they were no longer allowed to attend at school. They would all go up to the third floor (Ruthie was included, of course), play records, and had a terrific few hours dancing to the music. Within those cramped quarters, they could forget for a little while that a hostile world existed just inches beyond them. Yes, Inge thought, *this was not so bad at all.*

The portrait Inge (left) and Ruthie (right) had taken that day.

But she was not prepared for the night Ruthie came home with tears in her eyes.

"Oh no, Ruthie, tell me, what is it?"

Inge was not sure she really wanted to know. The fear she had felt once before, on the morning of Kristallnacht when she was told that the SA officers were coming for them, now returned. She sensed that her life was about to take a turn for the worse as she gripped at her heart awaiting what Ruthie was going to say.

"Oh, Inge, I'm so frightened," she began, as Inge took her cousin's hand in her own. "We just received word that we are to collect our things and that we must go in two weeks."

"What do you mean 'go'?" Inge pressed her. Was she going to be able to get to America after all? Oh, she would miss her terribly, but at least Inge could relax in the knowledge that she would be safe.

"I don't know where exactly," Ruthie said, as she took a tissue out from her sleeve and dabbed at the tears falling from her eyes. "They are calling them the *Sonderzuge* (the special trains). All I know is that they are going to be sending us Jews 'out east.'"

Chapter Four

Last Transports Out of Bremen

Inge (left) and Ruthie (right) in front of Das Judenhaus *in* their coordinating handmade overalls.

"Going to the east won't be that bad," Inge said to Ruthie. "At least we'll still be together." Having uttered those words so many times lately, not only to herself, but to others, Inge was

beginning to believe them. She was right, of course, so she thought, as she did her best to stifle her nagging fears. *Wasn't that the only thing that mattered?* Although the Nazis had taken away their citizenships, livelihoods, and homes, she was able to remain positive because all of her family was still there with her. This, at least, wasn't like the time they had taken her father away right after Kristallnacht, now that was unendurable.

Although Inge didn't know it that evening late in the autumn of 1941, when Ruthie told her with tears in her eyes that her family was scheduled to be sent out on the next transport, she, too, was to be on that same one. It turned out that Carl had also received such a notice regarding his family, as did Frau Goldschmidt, Inge's employer, as well as all of the younger families with children in the Judenhaus. They were told the specific day and time to be at the holding station. The older people were supposedly being kept behind, so those who were stronger could prepare the new "settlements" for their arrival. At least that was what everyone was led to believe. They were further informed to limit themselves to just a single suitcase, aside from whatever else they could carry by hand. All other belongings were to be left behind. Their money had already been confiscated by the Nazis, all of which was supposedly going to be redistributed to them from time to time at the new "settlements." Given just the few items that they would be allowed to take with them, packing for this journey wasn't going to be a major undertaking.

"At least we'll still all be together," Inge consoled herself as she sat on the floor in the room she shared with her parents, trying to decide what to pack. She neatly folded her woolen sweater and debated whether to put her warmest coat in the suitcase or to just wear it. She recalled that, when Herr Beiser came back from Poland, he told them about how cold the winters had been. While selecting some clothing for each season, she put in mostly those items that would keep her warm during the bone-chilling Eastern European winters.

Upon finishing her packing, she grabbed her thick ankle boots and went to the kitchen. Some knowledgeable friends had told her that the leather should be treated with a polish made from cooking fat to keep them waterproof. As she walked past the closet still filled with her clothing, she couldn't help but feel a twinge of sadness about all she would be leaving behind. True, there were dresses she would no longer have any special occasions to wear; but it was the clothing she had designed and sewn herself with Ruthie that really bothered her. She knew it was silly to get emotional over rompers, blouses, and the like. But she could not help but go over to touch the strip of mink on the navy-blue pillbox hat sitting there, in lone splendor, on the shelf just above her hanging clothes. Her throat closed, and tears formed at the corners of her eyes. Then she quickly scolded herself for allowing these silly little nothings to take such a powerful hold over her. After all, this wasn't the first time she was being forced to move or to leave things behind. Abruptly shutting the closet door, she continued on downstairs to the kitchen. *Why should it be any different this time?*

Her mother spent much of her time nowadays in the kitchen. Inge could usually find her there either cooking or preparing something. Such little rituals of normal everyday life appeared to comfort Marianne. In front of a cutting board, or mixing ingredients, she could almost pretend that her life was proceeding as it always had. She couldn't get herself to face reality without risking the possibility of falling into a state of depression. Looking at her mother then, as Inge treated the heavy brown leather of her boots, reminded her of a caterpillar transforming itself by creating a cocoon. There she was, protected and safe, still technically a part of the outside world, but too removed by her various activities to be concerned with it. Inge's mother wanted only her husband to tell her the specific tasks that she was to perform and absolutely nothing more. Inge, recognizing this, had come to realize that from then on she had to be careful to always appear strong and unwavering whenever she was around her mother.

Preparing to leave the Judenhaus was not at all complicated. A few remaining items needed to be packed; family photographs in their frames and the prayer book her mother received as a wedding gift would be the last things to add. What was most difficult was dreading what terrible place they might be going to.

They still had no idea where that would be, or what it was they would be doing once they arrived. That was why it came as such a surprise when they were notified just two days before the transport was scheduled to leave that they would not be going.

The Gestapo's letter indicated that Carl was needed to care for the elderly who were to be transported at a later date. Herr Platzer, the co-leader with Carl of the Bremen Jewish Community, was none too happy to find out that he and his wife were to go in his stead. They made a fuss, protesting in vain, but the Gestapo remained undeterred. The Platzers then had no choice but to quickly settle their things and pack up their household in a hurry. All the while, Inge wondered how best to break this change of events to Ruthie.

"Don't worry," she said to her cousin, as they sat together for the last time on the chaise lounge that had been serving as Inge's bed for these past several months. "We'll soon be there, too, maybe even on the very next transport," Inge stated with as much conviction as she could generate. She hoped that Ruthie wouldn't detect any doubt in her words.

"I hope you are right," Ruthie replied. "But let's be together the entire time until I have to leave."

That was fine with Inge.

Ruthie had her last dinner with Inge's family and brought over her toiletries and a change of clothing so she could also spend the night with them. The two girls squeezed together to fit on the narrow chaise lounge and tried not to giggle too loudly when one or the other began slipping off. Inge's parents were already asleep, so the two girls did their best to keep their whispers barely above a hush.

"I have a great idea," Ruthie proposed with some excitement. "I'll just stay here with you and say I'm your sister. I'll be careful to call Onkel Carl and Tante Marianne Vati and Mutti, and no one will ever be the wiser. That way we can remain together!"

Inge thought that was a great idea, and, as they drifted off to sleep, they indulged themselves in believing that they could pull it off. But by the morning, they both realized that were Ruthie to choose to stay behind with Inge's family, instead of going with hers on the transport, it would break her parents' and sister's hearts. Later that day, Inge went to the Jewish Community Center and applied to be a volunteer to assist those leaving on the transport. She was accepted and received a white armband that permitted her access to the area where the Jews on the transport were to gather as well as to the train platform, so that she could be there to see Ruthie and her family off.

As a volunteer, Inge was assigned the task of bringing a basket filled with loaves of bread for those going on the transport. The Gestapo hadn't informed anyone as to how long they would be on the train, and Inge was determined to hand out as many loaves as possible —even more than enough for their journey to the "East." Nine hundred persons, she was told, were scheduled to leave the next day on that transport.

It was already getting dark, when Inge was informed that all of the families scheduled to depart were already gathered in the local school's gymnasium, in the holding area. It wasn't a great distance, but it felt that way to her, as she hastened there as fast as she could, as did the other volunteers to that high school situated next to the train station. As she passed the front yard of the three-story stone building, the Schule Am Barkhof, she could see that many families were still milling about, waiting to enter. As a special volunteer, Inge was allowed to pass in front of them. When she approached the guard processing those who would be departing, upon seeing her armband, he allowed her to enter.

Once past the entranceway, she was startled by what she saw. Everywhere people were huddled about, in the halls, or else seated in small clusters upon the floor. The cacophony was endless, many were sobbing, some rather quiet, while still others were hysterical. Some people were voicing words of comfort to others, and there were also those shouting angrily, uttering grievances at the situation and about being treated like cattle. "Are we not human?" Inge heard one of them cry out. During all this chaos, Inge found herself momentarily out of breath. She felt lightheaded and almost lost her balance. "Oh my G-d," she said to herself, all the while gasping for air. "This is awful!" Something she was now admitting to herself for the first time.

Bremen Jews arriving at the Schule Am Barkoff School the night before being transported. This was the one Ruthie and her family were also on. At the top left of this photo, Carl Katz, in hat, can be seen waiting to see his relatives off as well as to assist the others who were about to leave.

"I must find Ruthie," she said to no one in particular, as the reality of what was going on finally struck her.

She wandered through the many huddled groups, until eventually spotting the wire-rimmed glasses and thick wavy hair of her cousin. As Inge made her way toward her, their eyes met, and Ruthie threw her arms around her dearest friend.

As everyone anxiously awaited their departure that night, it seemed that no one could sleep. Everyone spent the passing hours either speculating on their destination, talking to others to see whether they had any more information, or else keeping their crying children as calm and comfortable as possible as all lay upon the gymnasium's hard floor. Inge and those in Ruthie's family tried their best to eat the sandwiches they had brought along with them for dinner. But all of them were too nervous to have much of an appetite. As they awaited the transport, Inge assured Ruthie again and again that they would soon be together and that everything would then be okay.

As the morning sun entered through the gymnasium's windows, unlike all the noise of the previous evening, now there was an eerie silence. The only sounds to be heard, aside from the Gestapo's orders to start moving, were the footsteps of the Jews walking slowly across the wooden floors while carrying their few remaining possessions.

Although they weren't very far from the train station, it was taking considerably longer than the Nazi's had anticipated. They hadn't taken into consideration the slower pace of children and people hauling heavy luggage.

"Hurry up! The train is about to leave!" the German officers in charge kept shouting.

Those about to board did their best to quicken their pace. Many grasped onto the metal banisters leading up the concrete staircase of the back entrance, since they were prohibited from entering through the main passageway. All the while, the officers continued yelling at them to hurry. Inge at that point quickly hugged her aunt, uncle, and cousins good-bye, especially Ruthie. "I will see you soon," Inge said firmly to reassure her as she looked straight into her eyes.

The railway conductor blew his whistle signaling for the train to fire up its engine. Thick black smoke began to fill the already overcast sky as it prepared to haul everyone away. There wasn't even enough time for Inge to pass out all the bread. She and other volunteers started throwing the loaves through the train's windows into the outstretched arms of those aboard. The train started to depart just as her basket was almost empty. Ruthie and her family stuck their heads out of a window, and all frantically waved their good-byes.

"See you soon!" Inge shouted back as loudly as possible, even when they were now almost out of view. A blustery wind had blown Ruthie's long brown hair across her face, which disappointed Inge, as she wanted to gaze upon it one more time. She wanted to take specific notice of Ruthie's small, round chin, the oval shape of her brown eyes, and the very straight slope of her nose. She hoped to fix that in her mind so she would never forget how her cousin looked at that moment.

Even after the train had completely disappeared from view, Inge along with the other volunteers continued to remain on the platform. No one spoke. It was only then that Inge became aware that people were observing her. Those standing opposite, on the adjacent platform, were all the German gentiles with briefcases or groceries, going about their usual, daily business. When Inge made eye contact with some of them, they looked elsewhere, turned away, or opened up newspapers.

One young volunteer, standing next to Inge, wiped tears from her eyes as she asked, "Do you think we will ever see them again?" After hesitating, while trying to get herself to admit it, she responded, "I honestly don't know."

Inge wasn't ready yet to get on with her day, even though the other volunteers had collected their baskets and started heading back to the Jewish Community Center. She remained there for a long while, just sitting on one of the wood and metal benches not very far from where she had last been with Ruthie. The skies were overcast, and a harsh damp wind was blowing. Still, she stayed there, allowing all those Germans on the platform, those permitted the dignity of entering the Bremen train station through its main entrance, to continue pretending not to have seen what had just taken place—and to continue pretending not to know what was happening to these Jews.

When Inge finally returned to the Judenhaus, it felt empty and still. All the young couples and the families with children were no longer there. The only ones left were her family, Frau Aronstein, the older Horowitz couple, the Hertzes, and the two older men living downstairs. Carl estimated that only about two hundred Jews, down from an estimated two thousand, were left in all of Bremen.

By the following week, however, the Judenhaus was again full, but now with older Jews transferred there from other Judenhauses. Frau Aronstein, who had received her papers earlier but was waiting for her mother to be ready to depart, was finally able to leave for America, so Frau Ostro took her old room. The Jewish Community Center was then totally shut down because there were no longer very many Jews left in need of care and assistance. The entire operation was then reduced to a single office, located in one of the rooms of the Judenhaus that the Franks, one of the families sent on the transport, had occupied. Oma Rosa was now also there, having been among those forced to move, too. That gave Inge and her mother some comfort. Up until then, she had been staying with Marianne's brother, Inge's uncle, Hugo, and his wife. But they were sent to the east on that same transport as Ruthie's family, so her return was actually bittersweet for the Katz family.

With Inge's employer, Frau Goldschmidt, now in one of the "settlements," Inge looked for other employment. But the only job she could find was working at the office in the Judenhaus to assist the remaining elderly. She even began to learn how to use a typewriter, although she never managed to type with more than her two index fingers. Mostly, she was given the task of transporting all official documents. She became responsible for taking papers to and from the German authorities to the Jews still scattered among the few remaining Judenhauses. These documents consisted mostly of forms in need of signatures to transfer the few remaining Jewish homes and valuables over to the government.

Inge would usually help the elderly in filling out these papers, and then she would go by tram to deliver them to the authorities. Jews were now forbidden to ride the trams, but she had been given a special card permitting her access because of the "official business" she was carrying out.

As ever, the Katz family attempted to carry on with life as usual and maintain an optimistic and productive outlook. Each week, they drew a sense of security from their Friday night Shabbat dinners. Inge always enjoyed helping her mother in the kitchen with the preparations. After they purchased chicken from a butcher, they would then go through the process of kashering (salting) it before cooking. First they would cover the chicken within a large bowl of water for about half an hour and then lay the pieces on a wooden board over the sink, where they coated it with coarse salt for an hour before rinsing all the chicken parts clean under the faucet. Also, they bought bread from a bakery, Mohnzopf, which they would use as their challah (braided bread Jews eat on the Sabbath and holidays). While they no longer had their silver candlestick holders, they made do with tin ones. Every week, this was the meal where they would invite everyone in the Judenhaus to join in for the Sabbath prayers and to celebrate Shabbat as if they were still a fully functioning community.

Aside from caring for the few remaining elderly Jews, Inge also took it upon herself to look after Oma Rosa who was not adjusting at all well to the changes imposed upon them. Inge would often times come upon her sitting alone and crying on the couch in the room adjacent to her bedroom. She missed her home on 33 Isarstrasse terribly.

"Yes," Inge confided. "I miss it, too."

She would go on crying and fretting about her son Hugo and her daughter, Frieda, Ruthie's mother. Worrying endlessly about them, she kept asking Inge whether she thought that they were all safe.

"Of course," Inge replied. "I am sure that they are all fine. Don't worry so much. We will surely be on the next transport, and soon we'll all be together again."

These talks with Inge always cheered her up, at least for a little while. Inge would insist that her grandmother dress up because she knew that this always made her feel better. Oma Rosa obviously no longer had daily access to her beautician, so she now relied completely upon Inge to make her look presentable. They'd go down to the kitchen together where Inge first heated the irons in the fire of the stove before using them to curl and set her grandmother's hair. They usually spent quite some time doing this, during which Oma Rosa talked to her granddaughter about the same kinds of pleasantries she previously had discussed with her beautician. For that brief period of each day when she was being groomed, Oma Rosa could feel that the world still held some civility and order.

Ruthie's transport had left in November of 1941, and by the spring of 1942, the Katzes were still in Bremen. Inge never anticipated that so many months would pass before she would be together again with Ruthie. She found herself always hoping that life "out east" was going well for her, and that she hadn't been too cold during those recent winter months. In May 1942, the Gestapo ordered Carl to provide them with a detailed list of every Jew still in Bremen.

"Don't say anything about this to anyone," as he placed the list in Inge's hand. "Not even to your mother. Do you understand?"

She did, full well. Inge and her father realized that they wouldn't be remaining in Bremen much longer. As she waited at the tram stop on her way to delivering the envelope that contained the list of Jewish names from her father, she wasn't all that upset. At least now she could look forward to being together again with Ruthie and her family. That would surely be a change for the better.

Evenings after all her work was over, Inge often listened to classical music. The record player she used to dance to with the other young residents had thankfully not been confiscated. She'd play the Mozart selections, and the Barcarolle from the Tales of Hoffman on the record player that had been given to her as a gift from one of her father's non-Jewish acquaintances. The comforting and light-hearted spirit of the compositions also appealed to Carl. Many an evening they would sit together and listen appreciatively, as they each bore the burden of what only they knew. It was something that, even when they were alone together, they kept their silence about.

As they entered the month of June 1942, there was still no further German action. By then, Inge's birthday was also nearing, and she found herself focusing on that momentous milestone. She was particularly excited, as it officially marked her transition into adulthood. Her parents arranged to commemorate that event by having her father's tailor craft her first skirt suit.

She was so excited by this prospect that it took her some time to decide upon the perfect fabric. After leafing through numerous swatches of fine wool, she selected one she felt was the perfect shade of brown. The tailor then made her a sketch of a pencil skirt that would hit just below the knee, along with one of a single-breasted suit jacket. After that, she enjoyed going to the fittings, so that it would be tailored exactly to her measurements. Her mother even managed to find her a pair of shoes in a coordinating color and style. But they weren't just any old shoes. No, these had cork-wedged heels, were sling-backs, and had an open toe.

Inge didn't need a special event to wear this fine outfit. Rather than the usual skirts and sweaters she wore as an adolescent, she now donned this fine suit and heels to run all her errands. She also allowed her hair to grow a bit longer, so it now grazed her shoulders. But still she rolled the front sections back and pinned them up just as she had always done before her eighteenth birthday.

While Inge anticipated that the official transport notice would be coming, she was not quite ready for it when it was finally received. The papers arrived only a couple days after her June 24th birthday, and so all planned celebrations and fun were immediately cut short. It was a sweet reprieve, nonetheless, Inge felt, even if it only lasted a short while. But now it was time once more to be resolute and ready for whatever was to come next.

Chapter Five

Arbeit Macht Frei
(Work Will Set You Free)

Arbeit Macht Frei (Work Will Set You Free). These words on the top of the entranceway to Theresienstadt were Inge's welcome to her new "home." Appearing in a number of the concentration camps, this slogan was meant to instill in the inmates the idea that working hard was the best way to ensure their survival.

Herr Linneman had made himself comfortable in an armchair in the Judenhaus office, just as he might have done in his own home, as he waited for Inge to bring him a cup of coffee. After politely thanking her, he casually sipped away at it. Herr Linnemann was not someone who would ordinarily grab one's attention, Inge noted, laying her eyes upon him for the first time. His overall appearance was quite nondescript; nothing about him was particularly distinctive. He was of average height and weight, had light brown hair, and wore a grayish-colored suit. The best one might say of him was that he had a pleasant disposition, and perhaps that his light-colored eyes were indicative of a sharp intelligence. Otherwise, one might look upon him as an average, typical, German civilian.

Still, within the Judenhaus, everyone felt uncomfortable. After all, he had been appointed by the Gestapo, and he was there to constantly observe them. On that particular day, right before they were to leave on a transport, he surely had been sent to make sure that all of the Jews going remained calm and orderly. He was also there to make certain that nothing was being smuggled in or out of the house. Inge had heard stories of some Jews, in their desperation, committing suicide upon receiving notices that they were to be transported. But that was neither Inge nor anyone in her family's way to act. That being said, rather surprisingly, they spent their final day scrubbing the kitchens and bathrooms in the Judenhaus clean.

One might find that to be odd, to voluntarily scour the porcelain tiles in a house about to be confiscated by the Nazis before they were all to be banished from it. But it made perfect sense to the Katzes. One must never even leave a dirty dish around before going on a trip. In this instance, they definitely wanted to avoid any impression that they, too, fit in with the Nazi stereotype that they were just a bunch of "Dirty Jews."

"Are you packing?" Herr Linnemann asked in a friendly tone, as he poked his head into Inge's room.

"Yes," she answered, as she placed another blouse into her valise.

"Your luggage will not be inspected, so be smart and put your money inside," he said.

"Thank you, but my father would never allow me to do something like that," Inge answered.

In any case, they had been informed that they were forbidden to bring any money along with them. But after she told her father about what Herr Linnemann said, Carl told her to do just that, to sew some of their money onto the inside of a pillowcase. Although she was surprised by what her father said, as he was never one to break a law, she did as her father instructed.

Unlike Ruthie, they were not ordered to go to the holding station prior to their departure, and they were allowed to sleep in their own beds the night before leaving. Perhaps that was because there were now not many Jews left in Bremen. That night it seemed as if Herr Linnemann was always prowling around, as if to make sure that no one tried to escape. To be honest, Inge could not recall whether she had slept very much that last night, or what she did that morning before leaving, or how she even made it to the station. It was as if she'd been in a trance. What actually transpired and what was merely imaginary all blended into an inseparable mix.

What did remain fixed in her mind, however, was deciding what she should wear. She did think she ought to wear her new suit when she boarded the transport. She would carry her new, sling-back heels in one hand luggage, with her coordinating raincoat slung over an arm. True, she didn't like that coat very much, it was a black-and-white plaid print with red piping, but since it was a last-minute gift from Tante Anne for her journey, she felt she had to take it. This woman was neither a relative nor Jewish but rather a close family friend married to a Jewish man. It turned out that, when Inge had no money left to buy a coat, Tante Anne came to the rescue with this one.

Inge, ever clothes-conscious, decided to put on her forest green leather jacket instead, which she felt complimented the hue of her brown suit far better. But on her feet, she put on the heavy ankle boots because they were taking up so much space in her luggage. Carl, Marianne, and Oma Rosa, too, were dressed in their finest, in a sport coat and skirt suits, respectively. They were not only in their best clothes, because that's what proper people did upon leaving on a trip, but because they had no choice but to leave most everything behind; therefore, it made sense to take the best with them.

In their hand luggage they stuffed a salami, sausages, breads, containers of soup, and water in thermoses, along with four soup spoons, one for each of them, that they had been told to pack. Herr Linnemann escorted the family along with the others in the Judenhaus through the back entrance at the train station and onto the platform where there were already close to two hundred others, all Jews, also being transported.

Upon entering the passenger train, they seated themselves on gray upholstered seats that faced one another. Finally, the train's whistle blew, the engines fired up, and they were on their way. As they left, Inge didn't look out of the window at the city of her birth that she sensed she was now leaving forever. There was no one left there to wave good-bye to, and Inge didn't want to see the faces of all the non-Jews standing on the platform who pretended not to know what was happening to them. She just sat stoically there with her family and kept looking into her father's reassuring eyes whenever any feelings of sadness swelled up within her. The date of their departure was July 24, 1942.

Since the number of Jews leaving from Bremen by then was so small, as most had already been sent to the east, the train was more than three-quarters empty. But because there was room for at least another 800, it also stopped in Hanover, about an hour and a half later, to pick up Jews rounded up there. Shortly after that first leg of their journey, Herr Linnemann suddenly appeared and asked Inge whether he could borrow her father's shaving kit, saying that he hadn't had a chance to shave that morning given all that was happening.

"Of course," Inge responded, as she handed him the brush, razor, and other items. Little did she know that Herr Linnemann wasn't going all the way with them, but that he would be getting off in Hanover.

When the train pulled into the Hanover station about an hour later, Herr Linnemann was ready to get off. Many people then began filing into an attached car and finding their seats as it was getting ready to leave. With his task now completed to make sure that all the Jews from Bremen were on their way, Herr Linnemann returned Carl's shaving kit just before leaving the train.

"Auf Wiedersehen (German for goodbye, until we meet again), Herr Linnemann," Inge called after him, still not fully comprehending the insidious role he had been playing. Only much later did she come to understand what he then said to her as he departed. He replied, smiling all the while, "If we ever do see each other again, you will find me hanging by my neck from one of Bremen's lampposts."

"What an odd thing to say," Inge thought.

Aboard the train, the Katzes all felt fairly at ease. They had brought plenty to eat, the seats were comfortable, and the toilets were clean and in good working order. Also, they could look out of the train windows whenever they pleased and could even spot a number of identifiable landmarks. That first day or so, it was clear to them that they were traveling through the southern and eastern regions of Germany.

By the following day, though, they stopped at a checkpoint stating that they were entering Czechoslovakia. "So is this where we will be getting off?" everyone wondered. Inge also asked herself whether this was where they had taken Ruthie, too, all those months earlier. But the train didn't remain at the border. Instead, it traveled on into the open countryside and continued on its way for quite a while longer. Once again, they all settled comfortably back in their seats.

But it didn't remain that way. It started getting warmer the farther to the south they traveled. Oma Rosa and Marianne cooled themselves with little fans made out of cloth napkins. Finally, they felt the train slowing down, as the engineer began applying the brakes, and then come to a complete halt. Everyone began crowding against the windows in an attempt to figure out where they were. Inge made out a solitary sign atop a wooden platform that read: "Bauschowitz."

"Bauschowitz?" Inge asked quizzically, as she turned toward her father. "Have you ever heard of this place?"

"No." he replied, looking somewhat grim. "Never."

Why would he have? It appeared as if there was nothing there. Nothing, that is, except a wooden platform and fields of grass extending in every direction as far as the eye could see. The only indication of anything man-made aside from the tracks and platform was a narrow cement footpath that led off toward the countryside. *"Could this even be the right stop?"* she wondered. But when a painfully thin man dressed in civilian clothing boarded their car to assist in ushering them all off, Inge and her family became more concerned.

"Leave all your luggage here!" the thin man repeated as people began stepping down from the train. "It's a long walk. Don't take it with you. Everything will all be picked up and delivered!"

What could one do other than believe him?

"Katz!" they heard someone calling out to Carl. "Herr Katz!" the man's voice shouted once more.

This time her father responded. A young man then appeared, also incredibly thin, and wearing tattered old clothing, like the man who had first boarded their train car.

"I heard you have food," he said upon approaching Carl. "Don't listen to what you were just told, and leave it here. Take as much as you can carry with you."

"How did you know my name?" Carl inquired suspiciously. "Dr. Simonsohn told me I should be on the lookout for you, and when I found you that I should give you that message," was all he said before leaving the Katzes to attend to others.

Dr. Berthold Simonsohn was a fellow co-leader of the Reichsvereinigung der Juden in Deutschland for the entire northwest of Germany and knew Carl through their mutual work when he came to visit the Bremen chapter. Carl tried not to appear troubled, but he obviously was, as Inge could readily tell. Before she could even ask him whether that meant that there wouldn't be enough food for them wherever they were going, Carl had shoved Marianne's hand luggage under Inge's arm to carry as well. Inge had strapped her own over her shoulder, and then she grabbed one handle of a large basket while her father took the other. They began walking as directed while carrying that heavy load of food.

Marianne, meanwhile, was steadying her mother on one arm, and an elderly sister-in-law of Oma Rosa's, Goldina Gruenberg, also on the transport, took the other. As the two old women stared at the seemingly endless path ahead of them, they became increasingly upset and flustered. Marianne did her best to comfort each of them, all the while doing her best to assure them that they could make it if they walked slowly. But under that already very hot, mid-day July sun, it became an excruciatingly long walk for all of them. Inge was not at all sure they would be able to make it to their destination, wherever that was. But she kept such thoughts to herself. She didn't want to upset any of them with her concern. And so, she and her father trudged on ahead of the others, although she frequently looked back at them with encouraging smiles.

From Bauschowitz to Theresienstadt by foot. Terezin. By Severoceske Nakladatelstvi. 1988. Image 34. Like those pictured above, Inge, her parents, and her elderly grandmother had to trudge by foot several kilometers to reach the camp that was to be their residence.

Burdened by three pieces of luggage as well as the heat of the day, sweat soon began to drench through Inge and Carl's clothing. There was no one apparently around other than those from the transport, a long line of Jews slowly moving forward, except for an occasional farmer working in a field. After about an hour, and still with no visible sign of any settlement, Inge began to grow increasingly discouraged. To make things worse, she heard distressing sounds behind her. Her grandmother was wavering.

The physical and emotional stress of the trip was now taking its toll, and Oma Rosa was having an angina attack. Quickly, Marianne gave her mother her pills and a drink of water from the thermos. But it was obvious that Oma Rosa was now too weak to keep up with the others. As Carl and Inge both tried to figure out what to do, Marianne, fortunately, spotted a discarded wheelbarrow not too far off the path, and in an uncharacteristic act of ingenuity for her, insisted that her mother sit in it. And that was how this grand dame, Frau Rosa Gruenberg, made her entrance into Theresienstadt.

After trudging along for over two hours since the time they had left the Bauschowitz station, they could make out the ghetto in the distance. Inge was soon able to discern its many structures. The place appeared enormous; with its outer gray and yellow stone walls, it looked more like a fortress than the picturesque village she had imagined they would be going to. As they approached its entryway, and were being ushered in by the now several thin men accompanying them, Inge saw the white sign overhead with large black lettering: Arbeit Macht Frei (Work Will Set You Free).

Once they passed beneath that sign, they could then see guards with weapons standing at attention off to the sides. As the Katzes and Gruenbergs followed the crowd, they were ushered into a dark warehouse-like building they called the "*Schleusenhaus*" (Floodgate House). It was very dim inside, and its wooden floors were rough. Aside from some long tables, there was not much else. This was the place where new arrivals were processed. There, they were told to turn over their hand luggage, as a number of civilians, also Jews imprisoned there as they later found out, sat behind the tables rummaging through each bag and searching for forbidden items, like cigarettes. Several men in arms were also present, but they did little more than occasionally look at what was going on, either out of curiosity or perhaps boredom.

After being scrutinized, all the bags they had hauled from Bauschowitz were returned to the Katzes, with nothing being confiscated. Next, they were told to get on another line and to wait there until it was their turn. When Inge approached to be processed, a woman seated with a form in front of her began asking questions.

"Your name?"

"Ingeburg Katz," she quickly responded. "Age?" she continued.

"Eighteen."

"Origin of transport?" "Bremen, Germany."

"Occupation?" The interrogator never looked up from her paper on which she was recording the responses. Inge paused for a moment before figuring out how to best answer.

"I have been well schooled in tailoring."

"Very well," the woman continued, then writing down some numbers on a small piece of paper that she handed to Inge. It read, "VIII/I – 678."

"This will be your identification number from now on," she said. "The Roman numerals indicate the transport on which you arrived, and 678 is your personal number. Next!"

Inge remained close by while the rest of her family was processed. A tall, fairly handsome man soon called out to all of them to get their attention. He remained standing straight as a statue just inside the doorway, with his chin held high. He seemed pleased to have everyone look at him as he welcomed them to the ghetto known as Theresienstadt in German (Terezin in Czech). The man was dressed in a brown jacket with equestrian pants and riding boots and wore a bright yellow scarf draped about his neck. Inge estimated him to be roughly her father's age.

"I am Herr Comitte," he announced in a definitive Austrian accent. "Your *Blockaeltester* (block leader). Please follow me." They soon learned that he, too, was a Jew incarcerated here.

Inge and her family did just as they were told, Inge especially, who was a bit more eager to find out where it was she would be staying. But as she stepped out of that warehouse-like building and onto the street of the "town" in which she was to reside, all her breath escaped her.

It now appeared that she was going to be housed in a desolate abandoned military base and not a bucolic village as she had been anticipating. First they walked past row upon row of two-story cement-block buildings on either side, all painted yellow, with sloping brown-shingled roofs. Then they passed by a small marketplace with some storefronts, all of which appeared vacant or empty. Herr Comitte led them on past still more rows of cement-block buildings and then announced, "Now we are entering one of the 'L' streets. We call it that because it is one of the lange (long) streets here."

After he led them a short way farther, he then told them to stop in front of a doorway numbered L308.

"This is where you will be staying from now on," he announced, then adding, "But the men must be housed apart from the women."

Upon opening a door to what would ordinarily be called at best, a hallway, he explained that this was now to be their "home." Aside from two windows facing the street, it was just a fairly large open space with a worn, wooden floor, and small rooms off to the side.

Inge and all of her family were too shocked to express anything at that moment. The women then separated from Carl, as he went to assist some of the older men who needed help getting situated. Everyone was just milling about in confused states, trying to figure out where the bathrooms and nurses' stations might be. Needless to say, none existed. Most of these poor souls were thinking that they must have been transferred to the wrong building. Surely there must be a special facility for the elderly with amenities. Thankfully, Carl was able to provide them with some assistance.

Amid all this confusion, Herr Comitte approached Inge and asked in a hushed voice, "What is a young girl like you doing with all these old folks?"

She replied, simply, "I came with them. They are my family." "Now surely you don't want to sleep with all these old people" he said somewhat enticingly. Then lowering his voice a bit more, he added, "Out back there is a narrow stairway, leading up to a very small room. It's only big enough for two.

Why don't you go there?" He smiled knowingly at her. "Oh, thank you so much for letting me know," she said.

He then left Theresienstadt's newest residents, and Inge went straight to her mother and grandmother to tell them the good news.

Inge and Marianne immediately grabbed their things as well as Oma Rosa's. Just as the man had said, there was a staircase out back, beyond a small yard, an outhouse, and a water pump. When they found that room, they laid down their coats side by side to serve as a mattress and placed their hand bags at one end for pillows. Comitte was right: it was only big enough for two, but the three of them were determined to make the best of it.

Upon settling in Oma Rosa and her mother and leaving them to rest, Inge went back downstairs to see whether her father needed anything. There, Carl introduced her to the Hausaeltester (house leader), Herr Loewenthal, a Czech Jew, who filled them in on what was expected of them and what they should and could not do. Each was given only a soup bowl and a water pail. If you were able-bodied enough, you could fill this pail with cold water from the pump to bathe in; the water, however, one shouldn't drink. The outhouse and the house itself also had to be maintained in a clean and orderly fashion. Herr Loewenthal distributed ration cards for food and bread portions to those who were strong enough to eat. But most were too confused and exhausted, given all they had just been through. Herr Loewenthal gave Inge and Carl their cards to hold as well as a large metal pail.

"Take this bucket over to the barracks and have them fill it with food for your housemates," he instructed them.

Inge and her father each grabbed one side of the handle and walked as directed toward the barracks. It was a large three-story structure, with arched windows facing onto a courtyard. To get to their destination, they had to pass among many of the inmates, and, although Inge kept searching, she was unable to spot Ruthie or any of her other relatives. By the time they reached to where the food was being doled out, there was already a long line of people standing outside the kitchen window with their ration cards in one hand and a spoon and pot in the other.

As they came closer to that window, they could see a man punching each card. The cook at the window filled each pot with soup. Inge quickly realized that the soup would have to do, as it turned out to be their only meal that day. She stared down at the murky, brown broth. Nothing else was being served. Turnips and potatoes were chopped into cubed pieces in the soup, but Inge could tell that they were not very fresh by their dark color and mushy texture. It was, at best, of the quality farmers might ordinarily feed to their livestock. It was seasoned with a bit of salt and pepper, however, and Inge, who had become so terribly hungry, didn't think that it tasted all that bad. As she stared at the initial "K" inscribed on the handle of the metal spoon she had been instructed to bring from home, while sitting on her makeshift bed of jackets and purses on the floor of her tiny room, and consuming that soup, it now seemed like her life at 33 Isarstrasse must have taken place in some other world, very far away and unreachable.

The bowl given to Inge for her food as well as the four soup spoons each member brought with them from home, with the initial "K" on the handle.

By the time they finished eating, it had grown dark outside, and the three women were all more than ready to get some sleep. Oma Rosa insisted that they all gather together as she led them in the children's nighttime prayer, *Hamalach Hagoel* (The Redeeming Angel). "May the angel who had delivered me

From all harm bless these children. May they carry on my name and the names of my fathers, Abraham and Isaac, and may they grow into a Multitude on earth. Amen."

Once she had finished, Oma Rosa looked at Inge and Marianne sternly, warning them that, "We cannot, must not, turn our backs on G-d. After all, we have only Him to thank that we are all here together tonight."

"Yes, she is right," Inge thought, as she began to even out the lumps in her jacket as she lay upon it. She was so lucky right now to have her own place, one that she only had to share with her mother and grandmother. All the others downstairs came here alone, with no family members to lean upon. She then went over to switch off the light bulb dangling from the ceiling.

"Yes," she said to herself again. "I'm so lucky."

It was barely light outside the next morning when Inge sprang from her room and went downstairs. She wanted to be sure to be the first to use the outhouse before other residents dirtied it. But her heart sank as she saw the long line of people that had already formed outside the one small wooden stall. In addition to their normal needs, it seemed that the soup from the previous day had adversely affected the delicate stomachs of most of the elderly. Inge could tell by the swarms of flies encircling the area, and from the stench that reached far back even to where she was standing in the courtyard, that many of them must have been very sick during the night.

She had no choice other than to stand in line like the rest and to wait. Most of the elderly were not able to wait their turns. As they walked away in shame after having soiled themselves, Inge sensed that this was a far more serious situation than just wounded pride. Their luggage still had not arrived—it never did—and they had nothing clean to change into and no baths in which to sanitize themselves. It was only a matter of time before serious diseases and infections would begin to spread. Inge was careful to place some old scraps of paper that served as toilet paper over the wooden hole before sitting. She realized how important it was to take great care to remain as germ-free as possible.

Inge then went with her family to the barracks for breakfast and in the hope that she would finally find her cousin Ruthie. The cook served each of them something called coffee, but it was unlike any Inge had ever drunk. Like coffee, it was brown in color, but tasted like it must have been made from corn. The people in the camp called it "Mucka Fug." At least it was warm, she rationalized. And when she tried hard enough, she could almost convince herself that it was good coffee. She also consumed part of her bread ration, which constituted the rest of her breakfast.

She still found no sign of Ruthie. She and her family began asking those who had arrived in Theresienstadt before them about previous transports from Germany.

"There were never any others from Bremen that came here," they learned, which made Inge's head spin.

"Are you absolutely sure?" she would ask again and again. Her father would press hard as he put an arm around her in an attempt to comfort her.

"Positive," others always replied.

She sensed that her father was trying to console her, but it didn't do her much good. She kept trying to keep herself focused and her head from spinning. She knew that she couldn't let things get the better of her, that if she gave up all hope, she might not be able to take care of herself or be of any help to her family in this awful place. She had to pull herself together.

"Wherever they are, I am sure they are like us, safe," she said as much to herself as to her family.

Although Inge was still hungry, she got herself up abruptly, as it was nearly time to report for work. Herr Commite had approached her late the previous day and offered her a job in his office at "L407." Upon arriving there, she encountered two women, Trude and Gigi, each seated behind a table. They had been expecting her and quickly showed Inge what to do. They handed her a registry containing the names of all the inmates from their district of the camp. It was called the *Standmeldung* (position indicator), which listed the names of all the men, women, and children and in which houses they were. They had to list in it every new death that had occurred the previous day (usually one or two per house) and all visits any inmate made to the infirmary. She then was to give this detailed compilation back to Trude and Gigi, and it eventually made its way to the *Judenaeltester* (Jewish leader), who would turn this information over to the commanding official.

Every evening, the Judenaeltester would be given orders by the German commanding officer on how the ghetto must look and what jobs had to get done. It could be anything from scrubbing sidewalks, to making sure that no blankets were left hanging outside after 8 a.m., to various production work. There were those in Theresienstadt assigned tasks that were actually of value to the German military such as repairing uniforms. Also, there were many artisans who made jewelry, souvenirs, and bookmarks as well as those who constructed wooden bunk beds. Every day, Inge would finish preparing documents that were later delivered to the Judenaeltester.

Each day quickly flowed into the next, and Inge marveled at how readily one could adapt to even the most degrading situations. Trude and Gigi were nice enough, and, fortunately for Inge, Commite was not usually around much; he was usually busy running errands, although obviously keeping his eyes on her. Each day after she turned in the latest death report, Inge would go about delivering various messages. Most deaths, as she suspected, resulted from diseases spread by the unsanitary living conditions, particularly from typhus and dysentery. Inge also began to keep a small leather notebook of her own in which she secretly began to record the first and last names of each one in Theresienstadt from Bremen, who had died there. Most of them had been in the camp alone, and this was the only way she could think of to honor them, that is, to retain some record of their existence and of their death.

On August 2, 1942, roughly two weeks after they arrived in Theresienstadt, Oma Rosa said she wasn't feeling well. She remained lying down all that day, and Inge went to fetch her breakfast while her grandmother remained inside. Marianne gave her mother the angina pills, and all hoped that they would begin to work. Inge thought that they usually took effect faster than they had that morning, but Marianne quickly ushered her out the door, assuring Inge that everything was alright. Inge then gave her grandmother a quick kiss on the cheek, as she did every morning, and left for her job.

"See you later, Oma," she said, as she rushed out the door. It was a typical day in the ghetto, with the usual number of deaths to record, order notices to deliver, and office gossip provided by Trude and Gigi. It seemed that Trude, an outspoken blonde in her thirties, had a wonderful Czech boyfriend who would always take her out to movies and restaurants. By then, of course, it was a long time since she had had any contact with him, but he was still on her mind. Inge liked Gigi better than she did Trude. She was a pleasant, soft-spoken woman, with pretty dark hair, who had also arrived in Theresienstadt with her mother.

"But you are so lucky," she would always say to Inge, "to have your whole family with you here. That is so special."

Inge couldn't have agreed more.

And that was why, that evening when she returned home from work, she was not prepared for what had happened in her absence. There was a sign on the door of her house, L308, which stated starkly, "Death." She wondered who it might be who had died as she made her way up to her room. But it wasn't until she heard her mother's sobs that she broke into a dash up the staircase. Her father was already there with an arm around his wife, as she leaned over the covered body on the floor where her grandmother now lay. "No, it cannot be," Inge grieved, before burying her face in her hands, weeping over the body of her Oma Rosa.

Shortly thereafter, four men arrived with a wooden plank on wheels, which two men pulled from the front, and the other two pushed from the rear. Two of the men rolled Oma Rosa onto a board and then carried her down the stairs. After they had placed the body on the wagon, they needed to make several more stops to pick up others who had also died. Those bodies were also put on the cart—the same cart used for delivering the bread.

Inge along with her mother and father followed the cart, Marianne still sobbing, as the men continued on with their collections. No others joined them. Oma Rosa was apparently the only resident with any mourners to pay their respects. Once the men neared the walled gates leading out of the ghetto, they couldn't allow any of the Katz family to go with them. That was where the family made their final farewells before the wagon disappeared from sight. Then Carl put his arms around both women and led them back home.

"But you cannot be here," Marianne said to her husband, as he went to sit down next to them in their room.

"What else can they do to us?" he asked, as he began to make himself more comfortable.

That night, they all recited the *Nighttime Prayer for Children* before they went to sleep. That's what Grandma Rosa Gruenberg would have wanted.

Oma Rosa Gruenberg
1874-1942

Chapter Six

Schmuel

Schmuel Berger, in a photo taken before the war.

During the months immediately following Oma Rosa's passing, the daily lives of Inge and her parents continued much as before. It left little time for mourning. Inge suppressed feeling sad and promised herself to keep her grandmother's spirit alive; one day she would allow herself the solace that proper mourning can sometimes bring. But, for the time being, she had to remain strong, that is, stoic in order to endure life in Theresienstadt. She feared that were she to allow any weakness to develop, the debilitating conditions of the ghetto would destroy her, too.

Inge continued working each day on updating death records and running errands, and Marianne and Carl busied themselves caring for the elderly. But given the camp's harsh conditions and inadequate food, their efforts became ever harder. Moreover, as transports kept arriving from Cologne and other cities in Germany, there were ever more elderly persons, many having been evacuated from nursing homes. Most of these new arrivals were placed in an enormous barrack, called the Kavalier Barrack, which not only housed them but maintained one of the camp's kitchens and housed the mentally ill.

To Carl's surprise, one day a man sent by the Jewish Council of Elders, all appointed by the Nazis to run Theresienstadt, Engineer Elbert, by name, approached him asking whether he would be willing to manage the entire Kavalier Barrack, "You seem like a good organizer," he said to Carl, "I have a good job for you."

Inge's father accepted and soon began running that facility. Marianne did her best to assist him. But having been stunned by her mother's death and her own inadequate diet, which consisted mostly of rotting vegetables and moldy bread, she was frequently ill. Still she did whatever she could to help, although practically every other week she ended up having to spend a few days in bed. It was then close to Yom Kippur, the holiest day in the Jewish calendar, and Inge hoped her mother would feel well enough to endure the regimen of that fast day, even though Jewish law would not have required her to refrain from eating and to be with them that evening in their secret prayer service.

Even though the Nazis permitted services in Theresienstadt, the inmates still had to obey the curfew. By early evening each day, everyone had to be back in the buildings where they were housed or else risk being locked out for the night. For a small period of time, after people finished their shifts at work and before the curfew began, a large group had gathered in a somewhat darkened space near the Sudeten Barracks. It was a narrow corridor close to an outer wall. Those present consisted mainly of older men and women; those younger appeared to prefer spending their free time socializing with one another. Inge rarely saw any of them at these makeshift services, but, one particular evening, she did take notice of an exceptionally handsome young man standing alongside someone who appeared to be his friend.

Schmuel Berger was tall and slim, with a fair complexion and blond hair. Inge was impressed with his fervor while he prayed and how meticulously he dressed. She quickly ran a hand over her hair, to make sure that she, too, was looking her best. She was glad that she was wearing her beautifully tailored suit in case he happened to notice her. When he momentarily lifted his eyes from his prayer book and met hers, she quickly looked away toward the man leading the services. What she didn't know then was that at that instant, he, too, was equally taken by her. Schmuel leaned toward his friend standing beside him and whispered, "Take a look at that really strikingly pretty girl over there!" before returning to his prayers.

That Yom Kippur was the first time they had ever seen one another. And because there were so many people in Theresienstadt, it was not likely one would ever see anybody in particular again. The fortress, originally established as a military base, was only designed for a population of eight thousand, but it then occupied over 40,000 persons, practically all Jews, many of whom would die there, mostly from infectious diseases, or else be sent to the east where most were gassed.

For such reasons, Inge was ambivalent when she found herself secretly dreaming about running into this young man. Now was not the time to form an impossible attachment, especially with someone who might not be around for very long. Given all she had endured during the previous several months, however, and most of all, her separation from her cousin Ruthie and then Oma Rosa, such fantasies were nonetheless very appealing. She also increasingly worried about her mother. Marianne was growing painfully thin. Although they all had lost considerable weight, her mother's jaw and collarbone were noticeably protruding beneath her skin. It frightened Inge. No, she scolded herself, now was not the proper time to become infatuated, and with a complete stranger at that. Still, it did provide something cheerful to muse about given her otherwise dreary and cheerless existence. *What else was there to feel good about behind the high, stoned walls surrounding Theresienstadt?* The secret hope Inge held onto that one day while running her errands, that she would bump into this young man again, remained alive. He was the one image that enabled Inge to recall what joy she had been capable of feeling before being imprisoned. But after two more months passed and not even catching a glimpse of him again, she wondered if he was still alive. She had already seen how many others had succumbed to the harsh conditions. As the old adage, "Out of sight, out of mind" portends, Inge encouraged herself to no longer keep her eyes open for him when she went about her errands.

But things did not end up that way. Inge was waiting patiently with papers to be delivered in hand, standing at a barricade the guards had set up. She was being prevented from continuing with her errands until a long line of elderly and sickly looking people walked past to be loaded onto a train going to the east. Inge heard rumors regarding these latest transports. Those in the ghetto who were not productive or otherwise of little use, because of their physical or mental states, were being taken away. No one knew for sure what their fate would be, but most felt that they were being sent to their deaths. As Inge waited for the convoy to pass, someone began speaking to her in Czech.

"I'm sorry, I don't speak Czech," Inge responded in German before even looking to see who had just been trying to talk to her.

There she was, face to face with the young man with the clear green eyes she had spotted at the Yom Kippur service. She was breathless. There he was, right beside her, and he tried to talk to her. Before either could say another word, the guards began shouting at everyone waiting at the barricade to move on, and the crowd behind Inge and Schmuel surged forward. The two were immediately separated; she forced to turn to the right and he to the left. Like a passing wind, he was now gone.

After returning to her residence later that day, when her father had arrived, he informed Inge and her mother that he had been made the official *Gebaeudeaeltester* (building leader) of the entire Kavalier Kaserne. That evening, after finishing dinner, their one meal for the day, they moved to a room in that building.

Carl was expected to be on call there twenty-four hours every day and to remain on the premises at all times. Their new residence was situated at the end of a very long corridor on the second floor of the Kavalier Barracks, which consisted of one very small room with a bunk bed and a second single bed alongside it. Aside from a small window facing the courtyard, which permitted only a little light to enter, there wasn't much else. Inge was thankful that it enabled them to remain together and also that now there was running water from a tap as well as a toilet down the hall. She hated having to use the outside water pump and, even more, using the filthy outhouse. At least now they had a proper sink for washing and a toilet that worked.

But not everything was a change for the better, as Inge learned that very first night. Their room was located directly above where the insane were housed, and all night long Inge and her family would be awakened by the piercing screams of those strapped into strait jackets. It sent shivers up Inge's spine, especially the continuously moaning voice of an old man singing *Bei Mir Bist Du Schein* (By Me You Are Pretty) throughout the night. Yet even all of that she would have gladly accepted were it not for the *Wanzen* (bedbugs) crawling along the cracks in the wood of her bed.

These tiny black-bodied insects would scurry through the bedding and nip her all over as she tried to sleep. Each morning, Inge would wake up to find numerous reddish scabs on her arms and legs. It looked as if a rash had broken out. The itching was so intense that she couldn't resist scratching, which made it worse. After a while, a greenish pus began spewing out from the open sores. An infection had developed. Her parents became quite concerned after she rolled up a sleeve to show them how it looked. Revealing an infection in the camp was like delivering to oneself an official death notice.

For some frantic minutes, Carl fretted about what to do. Then he stopped in mid-stride, took Inge by the arm, and led her outside. There was a dentist he knew from Hamburg who had been assigned to the infirmary. Perhaps he had some medicine that could help. As soon as the man examined Inge, he concurred, "*Ja* (Yes), this must be treated immediately."

"Can you help her?" Carl demanded.

Silence passed while the dentist silently weighed whether to part with the remaining medication he had managed to smuggle in with him when he first arrived in Theresienstadt. Looking back again at Inge, he sighed, then went to a back room to retrieve a tube containing some salve.

"Here, have her put this on it," he said to Carl.

Inge and her parents were forever grateful to this dentist; in just a few days the infection began to diminish. Every night, before going to sleep, according to the dentist, Inge should light a candle. When the bugs appeared, she was to quickly rid herself of them by utilizing the candle's flame. After mastering that technique, she never again had a serious bedbug problem.

Another two months passed, during which Inge did not once see the young man from the Yom Kippur service. But she wasn't about to give up hope. Each day, as she walked through the ghetto's streets to deliver papers, she would observe everyone who passed. Never, however, did she mention anything about Schmuel to either Gigi or Trude, as they were such gossips. The stories they told in the office didn't usually bother Inge, but one day she sensed that they were talking about her, in Czech, which she did not understand.

A friend of theirs then stopped by to chat with them. Even though German was the only language the Nazis permitted in the camp, the three of them continued to converse in Czech. As

Inge became increasingly annoyed and thought of telling them so, their visitor approached her, saying in German, "There is someone outside who would like to speak with you."

Gigi and Trude would often invite Inge out after the day's work to socialize, but she never joined them. At the time, she didn't care to meet any young men. Too much else was more important. Many of the elderly required assistance, and she preferred to spend her free time with her parents. Who knew how long they would still be allowed to remain together?

"Thank you, but I'm not interested," Inge replied.

"Don't be so rude," the friend responded. "Go and tell him that yourself."

"All right," Inge answered, peeved. After all, she supposed,

"I ought at least to be polite."

Completely ready to reject this would-be suitor, to Inge's surprise, there was Schmuel, wearing tall brown boots and a white shirt neatly tucked in waiting to greet her. His blond hair was elegantly combed back, and he smiled at her before even saying a word.

"My name is Schmuel," he said in a heavily accented German. "If you have some time after work today, I would like to invite you for a walk."

"Not today," Inge replied curtly, then lied, "I have too much to do today."

"Well then, how about tomorrow?" he asked her, aided by a slight smile to soften her resistance.

She looked at him somewhat more closely. After all, he did go out of his way to find her. She reasoned that anyone who prayed as intensely as he had must be somebody who was good at heart. Besides, she really did want to accept.

"Okay," she responded.

His face broke out into a full smile. Inge quickly returned to the office, saying nothing more. Without stopping, she walked straight past the two Czech women, who momentarily stopped their talking, wanting to hear what she would tell them about what had taken place outside. But when they saw that she wasn't going to offer them even an inkling, they went back to their tasks. As Inge began once again to sort through the documents she still had to process, she couldn't help but feel excited about her upcoming rendezvous. She began to muse about what she ought to wear on this, her first, "date."

She didn't have many options, she realized while rummaging through her suitcase filled with second-hand clothing later that day. As was the case with all the others incarcerated in Theresienstadt, no one received back the luggage they had brought with them or any of its contents. The only way they could receive any garments in the ghetto, none of which were ever new, was by going to the *Kleiderkammer* (Clothing Warehouse) and pleading for something. With her ration card, she was permitted to go through some of the apparel that had been confiscated from others upon first arriving in the ghetto. After one made a selection, that person was then permitted to take a suitcase to carry the garments back. That valise then served in lieu of a wardrobe closet for the duration of one's stay in the camp.

Nothing particularly appealed to Inge, but she finally settled upon a floral skirt with a white blouse. It, at least, was presentable, without making her appear as if she were throwing herself at him. One of the older women Inge was caring for was adept at making artificial flowers. She had given Inge a cluster of daisies made out of felt. Inge fastened them with one of her bobby pins to the side of her hair. *Yes, that will look nice*, she thought as she left the next morning to perform her daily duties. This was obviously going to be a special day in her life.

All that day she did her best to remain focused, but it grew increasingly difficult as the bewitching hour grew closer. With regard to meeting Schmuel, Inge asked permission of her parents first, of course. But they were most happy to hear that she would finally be having a pleasant experience in such a dreary place. They were also glad that their eighteen-year-old daughter would be spending time with someone her own age. As soon as she tidied up her desk for the day and had stepped outside the office, Schmuel was waiting for her.

As they walked from L Street to Q Street, Schmuel asked Inge about her life in Bremen before being sent to Theresienstadt. Every so often, he apologized for his broken German as he described his own background: he had been a student in Brno (second largest city in Czechoslovakia) before he had been sent to Theresienstadt. Prior to that, how he had grown up on a farm in Velky – Rakovec, a small Czech town, with his parents, two brothers, and five sisters. One of them, Perla, was actually also presently in Theresienstadt. Then he mentioned how thankful he was to have been able to secure a job in the camp's bakery, and, on occasion, given extra bread to eat. That last revelation instantaneously brought Inge to a complete halt.

"You are working in the bakery?" she asked, suddenly feeling some hostility.

Inge had never wanted to be associated with anyone working there or in the central kitchen. She was sure that she had made that perfectly clear to both Gigi and Trude. After all, she was not one of those girls, the ones who shamelessly offer themselves at any price, just to obtain some extra food.

Inge then announced, "I'm sorry, but I cannot continue to see you." Schmuel asked, "But why?" visibly upset.

"I don't want that sort of bad reputation," she replied, in all honesty.

He laughed. Schmuel found both her naïveté and integrity most appealing. Even though everyone was starving, the fact that she would rather protect her honor than eat confirmed to Schmuel that his initial impression of her was correct. Unlike many others, Inge Katz was someone special.

"Don't worry about that with me," he said sincerely. "Hmm," she replied before continuing their walk, "...we will see."

As he left Inge at her door that night, after shaking her hand, he asked whether he might see her again in a few days. He didn't want to wait that long, but neither did he care to make the same mistake of presuming she had no plans for the very next evening, to which Inge replied, "Yes."

Schmuel was relieved. He already sensed that this was to be the woman for him. But he could also see, especially after meeting Marianne, that they were in desperate need of extra food. When he showed up at the doorway a few days later to see Inge, he brought a small loaf of bread with him for the family. She refused to take it, suspecting that he had probably stolen it.

"They give us extras," he claimed, "and we usually eat them in the bakery. Please take this, if not for you, then for your parents."

Inge considered his offer, and knowing how weak and thin Marianne had become, decided to accept it. After bringing the loaf in for her mother, she went out again for another sure to be enjoyable evening with Schmuel. She even got to meet some of his friends that time, along with his sister. In those two hours between work and curfew, she found herself beginning to enjoy life again.

A more tolerable existence became hers, at least for the following several weeks. She began looking forward to spending more time with Schmuel and his friends, which made her workdays easier to endure. Now the daily burden of recording all the names of the dead was no longer the primary focus of her day. In Theresienstadt, where so many died each day, she found herself feeling more positive and remembering how good it felt to be alive.

It was soon again June 24, but that year, 1943, Inge tried to forget that it was her nineteenth birthday. She could hardly believe that it was now almost a full year since she had first set foot in Theresienstadt. She hated the thought that she would have to celebrate such an important event behind these menacing walls. In fact, she didn't even like the idea of celebrating another birthday at all. But Schmuel insisted and managed to be off from the bakery that day in order to spend it with her. She appreciated that gesture, but who could possibly think of something as frivolous as a birthday in such an awful time?

When he arrived to meet her that day, he had a mischievous twinkle in his eye. She was intrigued by it but also apprehensive. The Nazis didn't tolerate even the slightest mischief. Quickly, Schmuel ushered her up to the *cumbaleck* (attic space) at Q 211 that he shared with several others.

"I have something special for you," he whispered. "Schmuel," Inge replied in an equally low voice, nervously looking about. "What have you done?"

He reached into his knapsack and pulled out a cake he had arranged for someone to bake especially for her.

Inge gasped. "How did you get that?"

"Wait," he responded, smiling, "there's more." He reached for something beneath his bunk bed. "Schmuel, have you gone mad?" Inge blurted out, genuinely concerned, yet unwilling to tear her eyes away. He pulled out a very small flowerpot with a lone flower growing in it, a bright orange marigold.

"For you," he said, as he placed it in Inge's hands. It came from his friend Tevlovic, who worked in the gardens and had smuggled it from there in his watering can.

"A flower," was all she could say, almost choking on her words. It had been well over a year since she had seen one.

It took her a long while before she could get herself to set it down to share her birthday cake with Schmuel. Inge was greatly moved by what he had done and hoped that he wouldn't notice the tears forming in her eyes. No one had ever done anything so risky for her. When curfew neared, Schmuel insisted that she ought not keep the flower. Even though he wanted to give it to her, he knew that having such a plant was forbidden.

So many chances had been taken to give Inge this seemingly small gift on her birthday, and she truly appreciated that. They were most fortunate, though; no one had been caught. Occasionally, the Nazi guards rummaged through the inmates' living quarters in search of forbidden items. If anyone was found with such contraband, they would immediately be sent to the Kleine Festung (a solitary confinement dungeon). Inge had heard about the man who'd been sent there for kissing his wife. No one knew for sure what happened there because most taken were never heard from again.

    Still, Inge insisted, "No, I will keep it."

Chapter Seven

The Red Cross Will Save Us

Picture of the ring Schmuel had made for Inge with her initials, I.K. on the face.

Without giving a second thought to the possibility of being severely punished for keeping the potted plant, Inge carefully nurtured it. For weeks the lone marigold stood straight in its old pot, on the splintered floor beneath her raised straw mattress. Even with little sunlight coming in from the nearly windowless room, it managed to remain open; its warm, golden color reflecting that some purity still existed, even in Theresienstadt. That was, in any case, how Inge viewed it. Each day upon waking, she looked at the flower to see whether it was still healthy and strong. In such a state, it appeared as if it were telling her that, "Yes, Inge, this love is real."

But even allowing for such a symbol of hope was reckless, she realized, because it was not unusual for the German guards to raid the barracks when least expected in search of contraband. They would lift up every blanket and turn over the mattresses and throw clothing and other belongings all about the room. There was no doubt in her mind that it was only a matter of time until they would come upon her plant, and that she might then pay dearly for such disobedience, even with her life. Sometimes the Germans would even conduct raids in the same cluster of rooms more than once in a single week, and she had now kept that marigold in its pot for nearly a month. She knew that it couldn't be much longer before she would surely be caught. But by the fourth week, the marigold's petals started to wilt, and its leaves had all turned brown. Still having made a show of defiance, even in this small way, Inge felt good about what she had done. In addition, if only to herself, it indicated to her that she and Schmuel were meant to be together.

Having accomplished that, she reluctantly discarded this most meaningful gift. Moreover, if she and Schmuel were truly meant to be together, she decided that she must avoid doing anything reckless with her life. But it was getting harder, almost impossible, to find the will to survive. Death had become such an ever-present part of her existence that she was becoming progressively more accepting of it. Trying to keep alive was increasingly difficult each day, and sometimes it appeared totally pointless to go on. She never dared speak a word about such thoughts to anyone, especially her parents; she just wanted it all to be over with already.

All too often, she felt it wasn't worth staying alive just to be afraid all of the time: afraid of not having enough to eat, afraid of how skinny one could become. Some people actually looked more like walking skeletons than human beings; their eyes bulging in despair without even a trace of humanity remaining.

Instead of showing interest in anything, displaying any concern for others, or finding satisfaction in something, there was only a single-minded focus on surviving long enough to get their next "meal." Inge found it increasingly difficult even to look at them as she went about her tasks. To witness such degradation was becoming unbearable.

She was also constantly worried about her mother. While the extra bread Schmuel provided certainly helped Marianne, that alone was not enough. She had recently been transferred to work in "The Glimmer," a factory where she had to split mica into separate sheets. Frequent dizzy spells and stomach problems prevented her from going to work regularly. Inge was concerned not only about her health but that she would be labeled as "unproductive"—which could result in her being sent out on a transport. But some of those Jews who recorded productivity levels, did their best to cover up for such workers, and surely Carl's good standing must also have helped. Inge prayed that the Nazis would look the other way. Realizing all of that, however, didn't prevent Inge from fearing that her mother might nonetheless be sent away.

On that day in November 1943 (*why did it appear that the worst things always happened in that month?*), notices were posted throughout the ghetto, alerting that everyone was to assemble in the largest courtyard for a "counting." Inge grew particularly anxious. She was becoming less and less gullible. Her job recording deaths occurring each day sufficed to make her wary of everything the Germans did. The Nazis already knew all too well how many Jews there were, down to every last man, woman, and child. As they led her and everyone else in the camp out of Theresienstadt and down into the valley known as Bauschewitzer Kessel, she became particularly fearful as she looked at all the guards with their rifles in readiness to begin shooting upon the slightest provocation.

"*Just do it already,*" she said silently to herself as she gazed up at the morning sun rising on the horizon. She could no longer bear to hear her mother's endless sobs. Nor could she stand the Germans' cruel treatment of the elderly and weak. As all of them were forced to remain standing in orderly rows, the Nazi guards counted, then recounted everyone, and still did so once more. Hour after hour passed, as all were forced to remain standing in orderly rows and given nothing to eat or drink. Inge's feet began aching, and her back grew stiff, and all the while the many rifles continued to be aimed straight at their heads.

This torture lasted for an entire day, and as the sun set and darkness filled the valley, Inge couldn't help but note how clear the night sky had become. She could see hundreds of stars just over their heads. To her, they appeared to be a sign that a larger, better world existed out there, somewhere beyond the high walls and barbed wire of the ghetto, past the rifles targeting their backs. That distant world she contemplated that night, she was positive was orderly, beautiful, and peaceful. Such thoughts made her think of Schmuel and of the marigold he had given her. She was coming to believe that she had received it not merely as a birthday present but as a message from G-d that she was destined to love and be loved. With that realization, she forgot all about her aching feet and sore back, the many sobbing women and children, and the wavering elderly. Her thoughts became focused on Schmuel. She needed to search for him; he had to be somewhere in this crowd.

Then, German camp officials in charge of the "investigation" ordered everyone to return to Theresienstadt, "You must all go back!" They announced loudly. "Go back immediately!" Even though all the inmates broke out into smiles, expressing relief, it saddened Inge to see that. *"How far down have we all come," she mused, "that they have us seeking whatever comfort we can by tinkering with their evil ways."* Everyone, more than 40,000 inmates, started to push and shove as they began rushing back, past the Nazis with the rifles still pointed at their heads, and through the high walls and barbed wire to their prison. *"Why,"* Inge sadly said to herself, *"have you all forgotten so soon that you deserve better than this?"*

It was then that a pair of bright green eyes met hers as she looked about at the pathetic masses making their way back. The eyes forced her to draw her attention away from the hopeless and sad state of the Jews, her people. Those eyes belonged to Schmuel, exuding love and kindness as he approached her. In Inge's mind, he was her beacon of light and hope. Seeing him reminded her that they must survive all of this because life was still definitely worth fighting for.

She walked with him and her parents back into the ghetto and passed the kitchens, which had been closed up for the night. "It looks like we won't be receiving anything to eat today," everyone said sadly. It would have probably been only some brown liquid with rotting vegetables floating on top. But given what they had just been through, it would have felt like a banquet. Schmuel proceeded to speculate as to why they had been marched out to be counted, but no one had a good explanation. Only much later did they find out that it was because some inmates, who were part of a work detail outside the camp, had escaped.

By the following day, life in the ghetto returned to its usual debilitating state; as bad as November was, December was no better, even given the approach of Hanukkah (a Jewish holiday). In the camps about that time, the Danish king had arranged for packages with food and other items to be delivered to the nearly five hundred Jewish Danish inmates in Theresienstadt—packages, unlike many others, that were actually distributed to them. Inge had no idea what they were receiving, but her father thought some might include Hanukkah candles. What harm was there in inquiring whether there might be a few extra someone could spare, Carl said, so that he and his family might celebrate, too. When her father returned home one evening several days later with a small package in hand, they actually received a Hanukkah gift even more precious than candles. The brown wrapping paper when opened revealed a stick of butter. Oh! What a treat that was for them! Never before had they spread such thin layers over their bread, careful not to use it up too fast. That, in any case, was probably more sensible, since their stomachs were no longer used to processing such fats. For these few short days, Inge and her family felt blessed to have received such a delicacy.

It seemed like food was the only thing anyone ever spoke about or thought about. One of Carl's main concerns, given his responsibilities in overseeing the barracks, was maintaining the integrity and control in the kitchen. Food, being such a hot commodity, was often traded for other items and services. Given that it was always in such short supply, more for one meant less for another. Carl was often offered bribes for extra rations. While it would have been very tempting to take them, considering the needs of his immediate family, he never allowed himself to do so. His concern for all those under his care was just as important to him as were his obligations to his wife and daughter.

One instance of this was an offer from some members of the Jewish Council whom the Nazis appointed to run Theresienstadt. They wanted to give Carl a special title along with a position indicating that he was an influential member within the ghetto; that is, having become one of the "Prominent" persons, he and his family would be entitled to some extra food and a larger bread ration as well as better housing. Carl refused. Any time the Nazis ever offered anything that appeared good, he knew that it wouldn't work out that way. While he wanted to be able to help those in need, it had to be done only in such a way that it avoided bringing such assistance to the attention of the Germans. He therefore turned down the proffered title deciding to wait and see how things turned out for those who did accept it.

Inge was finding that she, too, was becoming a valuable member of the ghetto community. She had no idea when she first arrived that her training as a seamstress would one day be of great help to her during her captivity. As things turned out, because she had listed it during the initial processing upon her arrival in Theresienstadt, she was to be called upon to utilize her sewing skills.

Along with others with similar abilities, they were told to gather at the gate to the ghetto one morning where they were met by a local Czech guard. As he unlocked the gate to allow them to pass through, they were counted and then directed to walk toward a nearby wooden barrack, all the while surrounded by armed guards. Even though she was then outside of the camp, Inge still didn't feel free, and she had no thought of trying to escape. It struck her that, although no longer physically within that prison, she and her fellow Jews were still very much imprisoned. A sense of incarceration, it seemed, had successfully infiltrated into their very beings.

The walk to the wooden barrack only took about ten minutes. It was a single-story, long, rectangular structure. Inside were fairly lengthy rows of sewing machines and sufficient light coming in through some large windows to make working there possible. They were directed to walk down a wide aisle paralleling the workplaces toward the managerial office at far end of it, where an ordinary-looking woman in her forties appeared. She immediately began instructing them on how to operate the sewing machines and other basics. Inge subsequently heard that she was related to a high-ranking Aeltester and thereby obtained such a sought-after office job.

Their work, she told them, would be to repair German military uniforms. For eight hours a day, Inge sat huddled over her workstation mending bullet holes, fixing or replacing torn zippers, and the like. Many of her fellow seamstresses were so highly skilled that soon they were also given the task of producing camouflage uniforms from scratch for the soldiers. Doing such detailed work, including making the patterns and cutting them out, hour after hour, left Inge and all the others with aching backs and sore eyes. Still, it worked out favorably for her because the woman in charge of operations turned out to be lazy, even though all she had to do all day was sit behind a desk and record the input and output of each woman. But even that was too much for her. This manager directed Inge after a while to do what she was supposed to be doing, without it having an effect upon Inge's quota report, which gave Inge an opportunity to relax part of the time.

Spring 1944 was approaching. As Inge was returning "home" from work one day, she saw a great deal of activity going on within the ghetto. A pavilion was being constructed for the children. There was a flower garden being planted all around it. Other new structures were being built as well. Inge became excited by these and other signs of beautification and renovation as she passed by them on her way back to her barracks.

Still, after nearly two years of being in Theresienstadt, she knew better than to believe that the Nazis were doing this to be kind to the Jews. Rumors began to spread among the inmates about what was really going on. It appeared that all this restoration came about to appease the King of Denmark after his inability to deter the deportation of hundreds of Danish Jews to Theresienstadt.

Hitler, to keep the peace with the Danes, fellow Aryans in his mind, decided to allow representatives of the Danish Red Cross along with a couple of others from Sweden and Switzerland to visit Theresienstadt to see for themselves whether all those incarcerated there were being treated humanely. Germany also did this to maintain its working relationship with the Swedes, so that it wouldn't disrupt Germany's ability to import ball bearings for the war effort. Thus, the Nazis permitted a contingent of the International Red Cross a brief visit to Theresienstadt.

During the following several months, the ghetto was transformed into what appeared to be a much more habitable facility; one produced, of course, by utilizing the back-breaking labor of its Jewish residents. Buildings were given fresh coats of paint, and barracks were repaired and renovated. Vacant storefronts were transformed to appear as if they were thriving businesses, as these facades were made to look like prosperous restaurants and butcher shops. Sausages and cuts of meat were hung in window fronts just before the Red Cross delegation arrived, and dining tables and chairs were positioned in front of these various eateries. Long-dormant restaurants once again had functioning kitchens, and inmates, selected from among the most recent arrivals who still looked quite healthy, were made to train together as a soccer team for an upcoming sporting event. In addition, auditions were held along with rehearsals for a children's opera to be performed for the dignitaries when they arrived. The musical, Brundibar, was also staged in a newly reconstructed community hall, renovated solely for this occasion.

Neither were the elderly overlooked in preparing this deceptive display of Der Fuehrer's (Adolf Hitler's) "spa town," where elderly German Jews could "retire in safety," thanks to Hitler's benevolent treatment. Even outside the ghetto's walls, the Nazis placed bridge tables and chairs near the small riverfront that ran alongside the fortress. On that day, when the representatives of the Red Cross came, some Jews were even permitted to play chess or cards with one another, as they appeared to be seated comfortably overlooking the water.

Before those selected to be part of this farce could briefly enjoy any of its benefits, something had to be done with all of the cremation remains stored in Theresienstadt. Once the mass graves outside Theresienstadt's walls had been filled to capacity, the Nazis began to cremate the bodies of inmates and then store the ashes in boxes, each labeled with the name of the deceased. By the time of the scheduled Red Cross visit, so many had accumulated that the Nazis were fearful of their being detected. To avoid this, the Nazis issued an order for an assembly line of able-bodied elderly inmates to pass along these boxes of remains down to the river where they were dumped. When Frau Abt, a friend of Inge's who was one of those on that line, was handed the box containing her husband's ashes to be passed on for disposal, she burst into tears.

There was not only the problem of too many of the dead to worry about, but too many of the living as well. During the month prior to the Red Cross visit, transports to the east also increased. Between seven and eight thousand were sent out, which, as far as the Nazis were concerned, would suffice to alleviate the problem.

Large numbers of the elderly were made to scrub the sidewalks just prior to the arrival of the International Red Cross inspectors. It saddened Inge to see those old people, many suffering from arthritic pains, forced onto their knees with scrubbing brushes in hand. For hours on end, they had to slave away until everything was clean enough to pass muster with the Germans. All the while, until the Nazis approved of their efforts, those scrubbing kept yelling at every passerby, "Keep off the sidewalks! We don't want to have to clean them again!"

Not only were many older inmates recruited into the Germans' effort to pull the wool over the Red Cross representatives' eyes, children, too, were given a role. Those who were allowed outdoors during the visit were cleaned up and given fresh clothing to wear. They were permitted to play with toys in the pavilion, having been prepared beforehand for what they had to say when offered food by SS First Lieutenant Karl Rahm during the actual visit. When handed chocolate, they were to respond, "Uncle Rahm, the same dessert again? Why do we always have to get the same thing?" Likewise, when he offered sardine sandwiches for lunch, they were to say, "Uncle Rahm, sardines again?"

But Inge didn't mind that too much. At least for one whole day, those children would be treated well. Surely the representatives would be able to see through such charades. The sunken hollows of Theresienstadt's residents' eyes and their slight frames would surely give the deceitfulness away. Children, like everyone else, were far from receiving proper nourishment. Their food ration cards, too, only permitted them to collect but one meal a day and bread only every third day. Since most were too hungry to divide what they received into portions to be consumed a little at a time, many ate everything at once. Such persons then went without bread for days at a time.

Inge, however, didn't have as much trouble controlling herself. Each morning, she packed a small serving of bread smeared with some margarine and jam to take with her to the wooden barrack for lunch. She left the walls of the ghetto for her job on days when the Nazis were filming the propaganda film about the ghetto, *Hitler Gives the Jews a City*, which was made so that no one would ever believe that the Germans weren't treating Jews well. The Germans forced Kurt Gerron, the famous Dutch Jewish filmmaker who had starred in *My Blue Angel*, to put it together. Once he completed the job, they sent him off on a transport to his death.

On June 23, 1944, the Red Cross arrived at the gates of Theresienstadt, but Inge did not benefit during that visit from any of the food abundantly displayed in the shop windows lining the streets of the ghetto, although she did receive fresh clothing to wear and was allowed to watch the soccer game taking place in one of the barracks' courtyards. While it was clearly a façade, that day it did almost make her feel normal again. Almost. It also made her feel good to see a number of the elderly she and her father had been caring for, who were condemned to living out their lives in this dismal environment, able to sit by the riverbank for a few hours. And she was glad to see and hear some children playing with toys after consuming a truly filling meal. Soon afterward, the food was all removed from the shop windows, and the chairs and tables in front of the restaurants were taken away, the children could no longer play in that pavilion, and the elderly couldn't play bridge near the water. In spite of all that, Inge remained convinced that soon they would all be liberated.

The day after the Red Cross visit was her twentieth birthday. Maybe, she thought, what had just taken place would be a good omen that the forthcoming year might be better than the previous. Hopefully she and her family would all be rescued, and then, maybe, she and Schmuel could finally leave Europe forever for a better life together in Palestine. Nonetheless, she did her best to stifle such thoughts, as she had been disappointed so many times before. But as hard as she tried to keep her mind away from such hopes, she found herself drifting back to them again and again. By the day of her birthday, all the dignitaries were gone, but more importantly, she was able to meet with Schmuel after work. They talked about how they were managing to survive and how determined they were to continue to do so.

It was then that Schmuel took out a ring he had bartered for with an artisan in the camp, that he wished to give to Inge for her birthday. Of course, it left her feeling most grateful and fortunate. The ring, although small and made of tin, had her initials, I.K., on its face. During their evening's rendezvous, Schmuel preferred to avoid talking about life after the camps, but Inge couldn't control herself. She was just too hopeful in spite of everything.

Near the end of September 1944, she retained her faith regarding the future. That is, until the evening of September 24 when Schmuel seemed so different.

"What's bothering you?" Inge felt she had to ask, even though she sensed she really didn't want to know.

"I have been informed that I must be on the next transport," Schmuel replied, as he stared at the ground.

Chapter Eight

Roses in a Forbidden Garden

The petals of this rose Schmuel risked his life to obtain for Inge that she has preserved to the present.

"But you are so productive," Inge pleaded, as she placed both of Schmuel's hands in hers, holding on to them tightly.

Unfortunately, being young and productive was no longer reason enough not to be sent out on a transport. The one on which Schmuel was informed he would be, was to carry 2,500 men between the ages of twenty and forty. Children, also, were now being sent to the east more frequently. Those still in Theresienstadt were told that it was because they had all come down with various diseases and needed to be quarantined; they were being taken elsewhere for the safety of all the others. While Inge knew for certain that neither the well-being nor the safety of the inmates were of any consequence to the Nazis, she kept such thoughts repressed. How could she keep herself going if she were to allow such thoughts to the fore?

"I know," Schmuel answered Inge, regarding his usefulness in the bakery. "It must be because they need us to clean up all the city streets after so many bombings," he said, wanting to allay Inge's anxiety any way he could.

"Well, I guess if that's the case, it must mean that the war is nearly over," Inge rationalized, desperately trying to convince herself as much as Schmuel.

"If you find yourself going to Bremen, you must look up the Bruck family. Herr Bruck was born Jewish but converted. So perhaps he is still there. Mention my name, and I'm sure he'll help you."

"I definitely will," Schmuel promised.

"And if you find yourself in Palestine after the war, look up Frau Ostro in Tel Aviv. She lives at Chissin Street #20. She'll know how to find us, and she, too, will help you." Inge gave him other connections. But the only good it served was possibly to calm her down a little.

"Thank you. I definitely will," he said again and again. Inge was about to continue with her litany, but Schmuel stopped her before she could get out another word.

"Please, Inge, relax. We still have a couple days before I leave. Let's make the most of what little time we can spend together. Let's enjoy these last remaining hours."

As she looked into his eyes, she knew he was right. There were no guarantees during this war time. The likelihood of her ever seeing him again was slim at best. As it was, surviving each day was struggle enough. To make plans for an entire future together under the present circumstances made no sense.

Inge realized that she had to reconcile herself to the realities of the moment. The two of them then continued with their usual walk along the route they always followed within the ghetto's restricted quarters. As they ambled along, they spoke, as they often did, of their favorite foods and inquired about the wellbeing of their respective families. But that night, before departing for the evening, she hugged him closer and kissed him for a while longer. When she reached the door to the room she shared with her parents, she did her best not to show her true feelings to Carl and Marianne.

Inge hoped that they wouldn't be able to see how she was suffering behind her teary eyes. How was she going to maintain any hope or optimism when the very man who enabled her to do so was about to be sent away forever?

During the two years since Inge arrived in Theresienstadt, inmates had been forced to lay train tracks between Bauschowitz and the ghetto itself. The Hamburg Barracks, situated close to the new railway debarkation point, then became the official holding pen for those scheduled to go out on transports. Once they had been processed and received proper identification and assigned an ID number, they were permitted to go in and out of that barrack until their actual departure. Schmuel's assigned number was 740.

On that fateful day, after Inge's work day at the warehouse was over, she headed directly to the Hamburg Barracks to meet Schmuel for a final walk. That night, being his last in the camp, Inge was surprised to see how sentimental he had become about the ghetto. He insisted upon walking past his old room in the attic and visiting the Schwarz Baeckerei (Black Bread Bakery) where he had been assigned to work during most of his stay in the camp. As they walked here and there, he related a number of his early encounters upon first arriving and how he was happy to have been able to obtain extra food rations for her family.

He led Inge to a small garden filled with wild roses just behind the bakery. It was surrounded by a high, locked, wrought-iron gate, and, before Inge could even think of trying to stop him, Schmuel had already climbed over it and had jumped inside.

"Don't!" Inge felt like shouting, fearful of who might have seen him, but only uttered the word in the loudest of whispers. "They'll punish you!"

He stopped momentarily and turned to look at her. There was sadness in his eyes but also a look of contentment on his face.

"What more trouble can I possibly get into now? I'm already set to leave on a transport in the morning," he said with a small smile.

He then proceeded to sort through those prickly rose bushes before picking the most perfect flower he could find. He climbed back over the fence. It was almost curfew now, and they had but a few minutes left before they had to be off the streets.

"For you," he said, as he presented the small, pinkish rose to Inge. He reached into his shirt pocket and pulled out a black-and-white photo taken of himself before the war. It depicted a smiling Schmuel dressed in an overcoat and wearing a hat tilted to one side. In the privacy of that narrow back alley the lovers made their final good-byes before walking back to the holding station in the Hamburg Barracks, where Schmuel had been ordered to spend the night. Inge waited out front on the street until she saw him poke his head out of a second-story window and wave. She quickly waved back and then began to run because she couldn't bear for Schmuel to see her sobbing. But all the way back to her barracks, she cried and didn't care who else might see her in such a state.

The photo he gave her that night.

That night Inge tossed and turned and finally fell into a restless sleep. Her eyes were still swollen, but, in spite of her loss, she did her best to act as if everything were normal. Her parents knew better. Even during the night, they pretended not to hear her sobbing. Marianne placed a hand on her daughter's shoulder before Inge left the next morning to spend another day behind a sewing machine, but that small gesture offered no relief. Nothing could.

That particular day, September 27, 1944, happened to be Yom Kippur. It was sunny and warm as Inge headed toward the wooden barrack to put in another obligatory day at work. But she hadn't gone very far before she began seeing smiles on people's faces, most of whom were talking animatedly.

"What is it? What's happened?" she asked one of them. "A miracle! Maybe G-d has answered our prayers on this holy day. The transport hasn't come. Maybe the war is over!"

Instantaneously, Inge was a different person. Her heart began pounding like never before.

"Schmuel is still here!" she kept saying. "Maybe this hellish existence is over at last. Maybe the war really has ended." But there was no way she could chance checking on Schmuel until the end of her working day, the hours of which seemed endless.

As soon as she returned inside the walls of the ghetto late that afternoon, Inge ran quickly to the Hamburg Barracks to look for Schmuel.

"Why are they still keeping you here?" she asked him. As ecstatic as Inge was to see him, Schmuel, too, was equally moved. However, she could see in his eyes that their happiness wasn't going to last.

"They haven't called off the transport. It's postponed only for today. We're now scheduled to leave tomorrow."

"You don't know for sure," Inge argued, refusing to accept his words. "Maybe something else will happen. The war could be over for all we know."

That evening grew cold, and they decided to spend their remaining time together indoors, with her parents, rather than take their usual walk. There, everyone talked continuously about what might be going on outside of their prison. Inge had trouble concentrating. The cold was getting to her, and her teeth began chattering. None of the others, though, seemed to be bothered. Right before curfew, as Schmuel got ready to leave, Inge insisted that he take her blanket for the night so as to keep himself warm in spite of how she was feeling. He refused, but she remained adamant. Seeing how much it meant to her he agreed to use it that night.

"I'll see you early tomorrow," Inge said. They hugged and kissed, not knowing whether it would ever be possible to meet again.

"I'll see you in the morning," he said.

When Inge awoke, she was still feeling upbeat. But that optimism quickly collapsed once she approached the Hamburg Barracks on her way to the sewing factory. Just behind that building, she could see a large black train parked with the attached cattle cars awaiting its cargo.

"No," she said to herself and began shaking. "We're supposed to have a miracle."

As if sensing her presence at that very moment, Schmuel stuck his head out of a window on the second floor and called down to her. He then threw down Inge's blanket and shouted, "I hope to see you again!"

Inge was speechless, but then, after swallowing hard and forcing back a lump in her throat, she managed to reply, "I hope to see you again, too," although hardly loud enough for him to hear. With tears streaming down her face, she bent down to gather up the blanket. She could feel Schmuel's eyes watching her all the while as she walked away and out of his sight. She refused to turn around and continued walking to put in another day's labor. That fateful day was September 28, 1944.

A train, like Schmuel's, arriving at Theresienstadt after June 1, 1943 to transport Jews non-stop to either death camps or to labor camps where they would then be worked to their deaths. Terezin. By Severoceske Nakladatelstvi, 1988. Image 154.

Inge had no idea what would become of Schmuel. Not even that he was going to be transported in a train car that didn't allow him enough room to sit or lie down, and that his journey would last for days. Only much later did she learn that nearly sixty men were forced to squeeze into a space meant to haul no more than eight horses, and that the only amenity would be two pails, one filled with water, and the other empty to be filled with human waste. She did not know then that, after that transport left Theresienstadt, it would not stop again for several days.

When it finally did, the door of that rail car designed to hold animals noisily opened, and they were greeted by groups of men in blue-and-white striped uniforms shouting at them, "Quick, quick, get down!"

"Where are we?" Schmuel asked one of them. "Birkenau. Auschwitz."

"Is there anyone here from Theresienstadt?" he inquired. "There were."

"Were? And where are they now?" "In heaven," was his response.

Had Inge known that at the time, she would have been horrified to learn that, right after being marched off to a processing barrack, Schmuel and all the others were ordered by SS officers to remove all of their clothing except their leather shoes and belts. And after that, they were forced to take showers but given nothing to dry themselves with, after which, all their bodily hair was shaved off from head to toe. Only then was each handed a shirt, trousers, and a coat and cap to wear before being led off to another wooden barrack. It was actually a converted stable whose drafty walls consisted only of rough-hewn boards. There they had to sleep on three-tiered wooden-plank beds, 15 men on the lowest, 14 on the middle one, and 13 on the uppermost. A similar arrangement filled the other half of the barrack as well.

Thank G-d Inge didn't know at the time about that and the dire conditions Schmuel would be confronting the following morning. After being given only a blackish liquid as their breakfast, orders were then shouted out at them to go outdoors for a roll call. As they stood there in rows, hungry and frozen, it was impossible for them to see the sun, which remained hidden behind clouds of smoke rising ceaselessly from the ovens in the crematoria that were always on. The stench from the burning flesh, hair, and bones filled the air, which Schmuel and all the others had to breathe morning, noon, and night. As the days passed, he and the other inmates found themselves developing black senses of humor in spite of themselves. They would joke about how they would leave this place and that the fastest, most surefire way, would be via one of the crematoria's chimneys.

Thankfully, as Inge eventually learned, he did have one happy occasion after being sent away to Auschwitz. An arrangement had been made with a kapo (an inmate selected by the Nazi guards to oversee forced labor details such as the one Schmuel was assigned) who said to him, "Should anyone ask you while you wait for me to return, say you've been ordered to fetch lumber for the camp."

Shortly thereafter, he was told to wait near a section of the camp where women were being held, and to his great surprise and joy, he came upon four of his sisters whom he hadn't seen in over six years. While he could barely recognize any of them, given the physical hardships they had endured, he was still thankful at having been reunited with them, even if that reunion didn't last for long. Sadly, though, when he had asked about what had become of their parents, he received the awful news that they had been gassed immediately upon arriving at the camp. His mother was not yet fifty, and his father was under sixty. Also, his eighty-seven-year-old grandmother, her sister, and a number of other relatives and friends also perished— murdered—and that their bodies were disposed of via Auschwitz's crematoria.

Schmuel could never have imagined that Theresienstadt, for all its degradations, would ever have been a place where he would long to return. As he stood outside the gate of that women's camp where this kapo told him to wait until he returned, with his cart still in hand, a small group of women, all clad in skimpy rags while a cold December wind kept blowing, passed by with a uniformed SS woman officer directing them. Schmuel thought of Inge. He missed her terribly but was ever so grateful that she wasn't there with him now. As he looked at the wretched girls walking past, he wondered whether there were any among them he might have once known. They all were carrying towels, but Schmuel couldn't tell if they knew this trek was leading them to their deaths. He murmured his thanks to G-d that Inge wasn't among them, wherever they might be headed.

Suddenly, however, Schmuel's solitary meditations came to an abrupt end as he saw an SS officer coming toward him. Standing there alone with the cart that the kapo had told him to watch, he was certain from the look in that German guard's eyes, and the speed at which he was approaching, that surely he was about to be shot. With no option but to remain still, Schmuel grew petrified.

His mind was racing. Was the visit he had just had with his sisters to be his last? Why did that reunion occur just then? Was it perhaps a heavenly reward for all the good deeds he had previously done? But before he could sort things out in his own mind, the SS officer pointed his pistol at Schmuel's head and shouted, "*Schweinhund* (swine dog), what are you doing here?"

Chapter Nine

We Will Never Be Separated

One of the actual stars Inge was required to sew on to all her outerwear.

For Inge, after Schmuel was transported to Auschwitz, every passing day was just like the previous one. Without him, she felt that life had no meaning; from one hour to the next, from one day to that succeeding it, there was nothing to look forward to. No more pleasant walks about the ghetto, no holding hands in their funny little way, pinky finger intertwined with pinky finger. After work, he was no longer there to provide his companionship. These were the things she had always looked forward to; they enabled her to get through each day in the factory.

The transports steadily increased in number after the one Schmuel was put on. The only thing that gave Inge some hope was that the wives of the men sent to the "east" were informed that they would be allowed to join them. Almost all volunteered to do so, and Inge prayed that this wasn't just another instance of Nazi treachery.

Often, Inge spent the entire evening just thinking about Schmuel and what he might be enduring. At first, she did her best to block him out of her thoughts, just to spare herself the suffering that losing him was causing. But even she, the biggest optimist in Theresienstadt, as she had designated herself, finally had to admit that his leaving was catastrophic. Probably she would never see him again. Yet when she least anticipated it, usually in the quiet of the night, Schmuel re-entered her thoughts. At such times, she would relive all that they had done together. Her memories became so vivid, she could almost trick herself into sensing that he was still there; that the rose he had given to her hadn't happened months ago but merely hours.

Such momentary respites were the only times she felt like her old self; the happiness one feels when they are sought after and loved. It was for that reason that she resolved to keep Schmuel's spirit alive within her for as long as she was alive and they remained captives of the Nazis.

Inge persisted in believing that the day would come when her one and only, her beloved, would return to her alive and well. She sensed that, were she to begin entertaining the thought that Schmuel was gone forever, it would be the death of her. With so many dying about her every day, it was easy to lose all hope. She knew she must remain strong for the sake of her parents, especially her mother. Therefore, it was most important for her to remain strong in her faith that Schmuel would be coming back to her.

The latest transports, as far as Inge could tell, appeared to be singling out those the Nazis had considered to be "unproductive." In Theresienstadt, everyone seemed to be ranked on the basis of their usefulness. This meant that those like Inge and her father, fortunately, ranked high, while others, like her mother, ranked at the bottom. It didn't come as much of a surprise when the day came that Marianne's name had been placed on the list for the next outgoing transport. That evening, when all were back in their room, the family discussed what they could do.

"Isn't there someone you could speak to?" Inge pleaded with her father.

"No, it's impossible to bargain," Carl replied.

What he actually meant was that the time had come when no one remained safe any longer. Although he was a leader of sorts within the ghetto, it didn't provide enough influence. But even the Prominents weren't exempt. Some of them, too, had been transported along with those considered worthless. Carl's initial reservations when he declined a more elite position now made some sense. More and more of those Prominents, who had been put in charge along with their families, had by then also been sent to the "east."

"Whatever happens, we must all stay together. That's what we decided from the time we first arrived," Carl reminded Marianne and Inge.

"No, Carl," Marianne interjected. "You must not." But Carl wouldn't hear of it.

"Inge, tomorrow, go to your factory supervisor, Herr Freiberger, and submit your written request to be included on the next transport. And I will go to the Judenaeltester, Herr Murmelstein, and submit my request to be on it as well."

As was always the case, Carl's edict was the one the family followed.

The very next morning, Inge went directly to her supervisor's office to do as her father had directed. Actually, she was in favor of her father's decision, as she couldn't imagine being separated from her parents. But when she arrived at Herr Freiberger's office, he wasn't there. She borrowed a pen and wrote a note requesting to be placed on that transport. Her hands were shaking as she folded the letter. Perhaps she had just signed her own death sentence.

Carl had told Inge to meet him back at the Judenaeltester's office, but it was virtually impossible to reach it. A mob had been forming; that is, all those who had been selected to be on the next transport, and who were there trying to get more information. They wanted to know what they should be taking with them, exactly when they would be leaving, and so on. But even Murmelstein didn't know. He indicated through his aides that he was still trying to obtain such information from the Komandantur's office, that is, the Nazis who were in charge. Inge finally saw her father in the crowd, and each began to edge their way toward the other.

"Did you speak to Herr Freiberger?" Carl asked.

"No. He wasn't there, but I did leave a note on his desk."

"Good," her father replied, although his eyes looked pained as he spoke these words.

Shortly after that, Murmelstein appeared, having just met with the Nazi commandant. He began shouting out at everyone to step aside so he could make his way back to his office. People on all sides shouted questions at him, all of which he ignored, saying only, "Please be patient."

It was then that Murmelstein noticed Carl. "Katz? What are you doing here? You're not on the list." He looked confused.

"I want to be with my wife," Carl replied, sounding adamant. The Judenaeltester was displeased hearing that and quickly ushered Carl into his office. Inge, however, remained outside, still shaken from having left that paper with Herr Freiberger, the one that would seal her fate.

Once inside, Murmelstein began arguing with Carl, "Katz, you can't volunteer to be on that transport. I need you here."

Carl understood that the Judenaeltester wanted to hold on to everyone he counted upon to help him maintain things as best as possible and for as long as possible for those still remaining in the ghetto. He counted upon people like Carl to make sure that whatever meager food, or other amenities they received, was because they were productive. Moreover, their labor was valued by the Nazis. After all, their work provided the Germans with jewelry and uniforms as well as other benefits at practically no cost.

"We all need you here to make sure that Theresienstadt continues to run productively," Murmelstein repeated after Carl indicated once more that he wouldn't consider separating himself from his wife.

Carl went on to explain his position. "We decided a long while ago that we would all endure the same fate together whatever it may be. Besides, my daughter Inge has already left a note on Herr Freiberger's desk. Please see that all of our names are on that transport list."

The Judenaeltester sat at his desk and pondered what to do. He felt that losing Carl at this time would result in serious repercussions. He realized he was up against someone who was neither bluffing nor attempting to negotiate with him. Once he arrived in Theresienstadt, Carl Katz had shown himself to be a man of integrity, and it could be argued that he held fast to his principles even to a fault. Right now was such an instance when he was willing to sacrifice both his own and his daughter's lives because of a promise he had made.

Murmelstein let out a deep sigh and sat back in his chair. "I will see that Marianne's name is removed from the list," he said. But just as Carl exhaled in relief at the news, the Judenaeltester warned him that Inge was now in great danger.

"You had better hope that Herr Freiberger hasn't seen Inge's letter, for he may not think she is as valuable as you are to me." Carl hurriedly thanked Murmelstein and rushed out the door. As soon as he saw his daughter, with both determination and dread, he looked straight at her and said, "You must get that note back." Inge stared at her father, trying to understand why he was ordering her to do it.

"Mutti is off the list. You've got to get back your note to Freiberger. Run!" Having gathered back her senses, Inge spun around and quickly headed down the hall.

Only a few hallways separated the two offices, and she ran as quickly as her feet would carry her, her heart pounding all the while. Her fear was so great that she wouldn't allow herself to pause. As the office came into view, Inge found herself going even faster. "Don't trip. Don't trip," she said to herself, as she knew that even a moment's delay could make all the difference in their lives or subsequent deaths.

The office was empty. But she had no way of knowing whether Freiberger had seen the note. Was he right on his way to add her name to the transport list? She wasn't able to spot where she had placed that paper on his desk. There were so many papers on his desk! "Oh G-d, I'm too late," she gasped. "What will I tell Vati?"

It was practically impossible for her to differentiate one paper from another. But, miracle of miracles, it was still there, untouched, and unread. She grabbed it and pressed it against her chest. Then, she leaned against the table and breathed a sigh of relief.

She placed her death notice inside the pocket of her coat and headed back to report the good news to her parents. She bumped into Herr Freiberger upon turning the very first corner. "Oh, hello," he addressed her. "Is there anything I can help you with?"

Having regained the presence to smile at him, Inge replied, "Oh, no. Thank you. Everything is alright," she said, as she made her way past him.

Inge, of course, didn't know for sure what life would be like outside of Theresienstadt, but she was happy to remain, given that her parents were spared from being on that transport. Like all those about to board that train, she never could have fully conceived of how dire and hopeless conditions in the "Death Camps" were. The fact that Schmuel was there, though, made it seem that it couldn't be that bad. Obviously, if she had known that it would have been highly unlikely for her parents to have survived beyond their first day, that surely would have made her think differently. Indeed, it was remarkable that Schmuel managed to survive there for three months after being transported from Theresienstadt, as she subsequently discovered.

Chapter Ten

Branded Inmates

A cattle car used to transport Jews to and from concentration camps like Auschwitz.

At any moment after being incarcerated in Auschwitz, no matter the hour, and for whatever the reason, however arbitrary, an inmate's existence could be terminated. As Schmuel knew, who was just waiting as ordered, for his kapo on that icy December day when that Nazi confronted him with gun in hand and no qualms about shooting him, he had no way to defend himself. His knees shook, and he could feel that his legs had turned to water, as that SS officer shouted, "*Schweinhund* (Swine Dog), what are you doing here?" at him. All Schmuel could think of doing was to try standing at perfect attention, with cap in hand, heels pressed together, eyes looking straight ahead, and uttering, "I obediently report that I have just delivered some lumber here on the orders of my kapo (here he made up a name as he didn't know the man's real one), and was told by him to wait here for his return, Sir." He rattled this response off in German and in the most military-sounding delivery he could muster.

That SS guard just stood there, not moving, as he appeared to be deciding whether killing this Jew was worth the bullet. Some kapos were considered to be of value to the SS, and perhaps Schmuel's was one this German would not want to have an incident with. The kapos, though also inmates, often were of special value to the Nazis, as they were frequently used to turn one victim against another, as these functionaries pitted themselves against their fellow prisoners to gain favor with the SS guards. This arrangement of utilizing some inmates to supervise others meant that the Germans could function and maintain order with fewer personnel. Many of the kapos were selected from among the ranks of violent criminals, who were also imprisoned, those already known for their brutality. No doubt they provided an important service, one that enabled the Nazis to operate the camps with less risk to themselves. But who knows what actually influenced this particular officer? Perhaps Schmuel's German made an impression, or his apparent military bearing. Or maybe this SS officer simply didn't feel like making out a report that cold day were he to shoot Schmuel.

Whatever he was thinking, this Nazi, after remaining there for several seconds, then turned on his heels and, without uttering another word, walked away. Somehow, Schmuel, managed to remain erect and on his feet. When the kapo returned, he didn't say anything to Schmuel, and Schmuel, too, remained silent regarding what had transpired. As he followed back behind the kapo, all the while pushing that cart, his only wish was to get away from that woman's camp as quickly as possible. The last thing he wanted was to meet up with any other SS guards.

This experience strengthened Schmuel's will to live, thereby improving his survival instincts. It was then that he began to wonder whether there might be a way to get out of Auschwitz other than via the chimney. Rumors circulated that those proficient in something had a better chance of remaining alive. One day, late in the night, those claiming to be a locksmith or mechanic were summoned to report. They were informed that laborers were needed to work in nearby coal mines. These inmates were then assembled and, after having numbers tattooed on their arms, trucked away. Schmuel couldn't determine whether they were really being sent to work, or whether this was just a ruse before being murdered in the gas showers. By then, he had learned not to trust anything a Nazi might promise. As he listened to those trucks rumbling off that night, as they passed through the camp's narrow streets, he prayed that its occupants weren't going to become more human fuel for the ovens.

Schmuel was then called to be in a "work" detail. Just as those other men had listed their occupations, Schmuel, too, had done so. In his case, he indicated truthfully that he was an "agricultural worker/gardener." Since he had spent his youth working on his family's farm, he figured that that might be the best occupation for him to list to gain access to food were he to be selected.

"*Raus! Schnell, schnell* (Out! Quick, quick!)!" Several kapos shouted, all the while holding clubs in their hands to use on any who resisted their orders.

All the inmates were then driven from the wooden planks where they were lying, about a thousand in total, from both sides of the barracks, and ordered to go outside. Schmuel was apprehensive, realizing that those kapos committed most of their bad deeds at night, after everyone was asleep in his bunk. Still, perhaps, as he hoped, this was actually a call to work. But his heart sank when he saw that they were not being lead out of the camp. Rather, they were being directed toward another enormous barrack fitted out with showers.

Upon entering, he could see that each washroom was fitted with numerous shower pipes capable of spraying out cold water or Heaven knows what. There were also rows of latrines. As they all stood there, and then ordered to undress, no one knew exactly what might come out of those showerheads. Would it be water for washing or deadly gas to kill them?

At the time, Schmuel felt certain that this was surely his end, and he began thinking about all those he loved who, as far as he knew, were still alive. His sister, Perla, in Theresienstadt, and his others, Rose, Gizi, Olga, and Elsa, right there in Auschwitz with him. Also, his younger brothers, Moshe and Wolf. And of course, of his beloved Inge. "Please G-d," he appealed. "Let them be spared. Don't allow any of them to suffer." Then, he decided to recite the Vidduy, a confessional prayer for one's sins. He even added sins he hadn't committed but might, someday, just to be safe.

"I acknowledge before You, Lord my G-d and G-d of my fathers, that my recovery and my death are in Your hands.

May it be Your will that You heal me with total recovery, But if I die, may my death be an atonement for all the errors,

Iniquities, and willful sins that I have erred, sinned, and transgressed

Before You, and may You grant my share in the Garden of Eden, and Grant me the merit to abide in the World to Come which is Vouchsafed for the righteous..."

As he recited these words, he could sense his heart throbbing and felt as if he wanted his soul to run from his body to escape this cruel fate. From where he was standing, Schmuel could see trucks moving nearby. Surely they must be here, he thought, to cart off the bodies of those about to be gassed to the crematoria. He was sure they were all going to be killed.

He could no longer recall the words of other prayers he otherwise knew by heart, prayers that he would have also recited. Schmuel felt so helpless. He closed his eyes as tightly as he could and attempted to envision the Hebrew words he had so often recited from the pages of his well-worn prayer book— all in the hopes to remove himself from the frightening reality confronting him. He prayed, having then remembered how to complete the Vidduy.

"Master of the universe, may it be Your will that my passing be in peace."

Chapter Eleven

Machine Guns in the Night

Nazi guards at the entrance of Theresienstadt. Terezin. By Severoceske Nakladatelstvi, 1988. Image 64

Life for the Katz family in the days immediately following that fateful transport returned, more or less, to the way it had been.

Except for another change of residence, and a new job with much more responsibility for Carl, Inge, as before, continued working in the wooden barrack. Each day, she would mend and tailor German military uniforms. Her father was now assigned by the Aeltester, Murmelstein, to the role of *Innere Verwaltung* (Central Management). He was now responsible for overseeing what went on in all the buildings in the ghetto where Jews were housed. Because of these additional responsibilities, they were moved to the Magdeburg Barracks.

That was the building where all of the Jewish officials and managers appointed to run Thersienstadt as well as other Prominents were housed. Because many higher-ranking inmates who had been in charge had recently been shipped out on transports, numerous vacancies needed to be filled, and that was the reason Carl had been selected. It definitely was an improvement in living conditions for Inge and her parents. In place of their single, small bare room in the Kavalier Barracks, they now had considerably more space. There was even a couch and a table. But, most important for Inge, she now had her own bed all to herself and not just a bunk bed.

After they had been there for nearly three months, something unexpected happened, as Inge and her mother were on their way to their respective workplaces at the wooden barrack and Glimmer (mica) barrack. Both buildings were engulfed by flames. As rumors spread among the inmates regarding the cause, the consensus was that it was because the allied forces were advancing, and the Germans, anxious to avoid having all the German uniforms housed there from falling into enemy hands, set the fire themselves.

While those fires were a great relief to Marianne, since she now had the perfect excuse for not working, the lack of work actually made Inge more anxious. She wanted to continue working so as to remain useful in the eyes of the Nazis; therefore, she decided to approach one of the bakeries. Because so many of those who had worked there, like Schmuel, had been transported elsewhere, perhaps there was a job she could fill.

Moreover, by no longer receiving bread from Schmuel, their need for additional food was becoming more critical. But when Inge approached her father to see whether he could use his influence, given his now greater standing within the ghetto, he cut her off immediately.

"No, I can't do that," he said sternly, in a voice that showed no willingness to compromise. "If you want to see if they can use you, you will have to do it on your own. The last thing I need is for someone to use any excuse whatsoever to badmouth us, or worse, to accuse us of having taken an unfair advantage."

Inge was disappointed but understood that her father was right. Obviously, he had managed to keep them all alive and together until then, unlike the fate of so many of the others she knew. But as things turned out, she didn't need his assistance after all. Upon approaching the Jew in charge at the *Weiss Baeckerei* (White Bakery), she was taken on immediately. And whom should she find there, actually working right beside her, but Perla, Schmuel's sister.

"Let's be friends," Perla said, as she placed a frail arm about her new co-worker's shoulder.

Inge was somewhat wary regarding Perla's warm welcome and wondered whether it was just a way of lessening her grief for her lost brother by maintaining this connection with someone who had been so close to him. She, like Inge, also found herself feeling forlorn after her own boyfriend, Smejda, was sent out on the same transport as Schmuel. But, after being together every day for several weeks, they started to develop a genuine friendship. Perla even began introducing Inge to everyone as her sister-in-law.

Work in the bakery was far from easy. Inge soon enough appreciated why it had initially been reserved for men. Huge bags of flour were dropped off by trucks, which Inge and Perla then had to haul into the building. As backbreaking as such labor could be, they both endured it, realizing that it ensured additional food, without which survival would have become unlikely. Still, with such supplements, they remained weak given their years of starvation and the resulting malnutrition. And so, these two small-framed, young women, in spite of their conditions, managed to find sufficient strength to hoist hundred-pound flour sacks onto their backs and into the kitchen area.

After they lifted each load onto the counter, they looked at each other with great satisfaction and could not help but be pleased at what they were still able to do. With cheeks flushed, and profuse sweating, they couldn't help but feel proud of themselves. *Who would have believed it?* Before they could even think of gloating any further, the baker in charge would call them over to teach them something new, like how to make the dough for rolls.

Once they prepared such dough, they had to transfer it into molds and press it evenly into one uniform size before putting it back into their hands to further refine the shape. Finally, the dough for each loaf was placed on baking sheets before it was handed over to the man operating the ovens.

Each night, right before quitting time, each worker received the reward that made that day's work worthwhile. To lessen the likelihood of inmates stealing, each was given a roll to eat, which everyone devoured right away—that is, everyone except Inge. While the temptation to consume the warm bread in her hand was almost too great to bear, she always brought it back with her to share with Carl and Marianne.

All the others found this hard to believe, but Inge wouldn't think of ever doing anything other than that. Having been surrounded all day by the aroma of bread baking and then having a loaf placed in her hands for her own consumption, she came to appreciate what a sacrifice Schmuel had been making. While she was always aware of his generosity in giving her family his extra daily portion, she now for the first time was struck with how selfless he actually was. Would she have ever been able to do the same, to sacrifice herself in order to help those who, at the time, were strangers? Inge wasn't sure. In her heart, though, she found herself thanking him time and again, hoping, wherever he then was, that he could somehow sense the depth of her gratitude.

The man who headed the bakery had only felt pity for Inge when she first approached him. But since then, he formed a genuine liking for her. He appreciated how diligently she completed each task and, even more, her devotion to her parents. As an indication of his approval, one day when a roll had fallen off a baking sheet and onto the floor that was being prepared for a Nazi dinner party, the baker urged her to retrieve it for herself.

"Eat that one now," he insisted.

But Inge refused because she wanted to save it for her mother.

Realizing why she was reluctant, he first looked about to make sure that no one could hear him and then said to her in a hushed voice, "Eat this one. I will give you another tonight to take home for your family." He glanced about, concerned that someone might be approaching, and continued, "Hurry. Do it now!"

This time, Inge did what he told her, picking the roll up off the floor, wiping it as best she could before taking a bite. She couldn't believe how good it tasted. The crust was flaky, and the inside was still warm. The baker smiled and watched her eating it with pleasure, which pleased him immensely that he could do something like this for a very nice, young woman. Unlike so many of the others, that was an especially good day for Inge.

Most of the time, however, losing Schmuel continued to plague her. She would find herself speaking to him, as if he were actually there, saying things that she knew would be of interest to him. At other moments, she would direct her thoughts, howbeit silently, to her cousin Ruthie. While losing her was not as recent, it still caused Inge much pain. It had been so long since there had been any news about her. Inge would always ask new arrivals she met in the ghetto whether they had ever seen or heard of her cousin, particularly after someone had apparently spotted her once in Poland three years earlier. But no one had. It was now close to four years since they had said their good-byes on that train platform in Bremen. She could still picture clearly how it was, as exactly as if she were looking at a photograph. There was Ruthie, leaning out of the train window, waving, with her long hair blowing as the train pulled out of the station.

Each time Inge began to reconcile herself to the fact that Ruthie was probably gone forever, a feeling of sadness would get the better of her. And so, instead, she mused about how she would describe Schmuel to her when they were together once again. Inge was sure that Ruthie would really like him, and she refused to give up the slightest glimmer of hope that after the war was over, a time would come when she'd be able to introduce them to one another. Inge, of course, hoped that Ruthie, too, would have by then also found someone special to share her life with. It would be so much fun for the four of them to be together and to become the best of friends. Inge dreamt of them strolling arm-in-arm along the streets of Bremen, or perhaps Palestine, all the while laughing and speaking optimistically of the future.

When Inge wasn't diverting herself with such fantasies, she found herself confronting the ever - precarious existence in the camp of just trying to remain alive. But rather than dwelling on such matters, she did her best to focus upon what she considered to be small miracles, like being able to share an extra roll now and then with her parents. All the while, her friendship with Perla continued to develop. She was definitely someone who could commiserate with the loss of a soulmate, as well as the loss of Schmuel, and life in the camp.

Inge managed to survive with her parents until the spring of 1945, unlike most of their fellow inmates at Theresienstadt. On an evening when they were fortunate enough to be able to share some extra bread three ways, they suddenly heard the unmistakable sound of machine guns firing. The loud noise resounded throughout the courtyard.

All three of them immediately jumped up and rushed to the hallway. Likewise, most of the others in that barrack did the same. Soon, those hallways were packed with people, all pushing to peer out the windows facing the courtyard, to see what was going on.

Voices could be heard outside of people screaming and shouting, and machine gun blasts from round after round of gunfire kept roaring away. But Carl, rather than continuing to stand there, after placing his arms around his daughter and wife, said, rather solemnly, "Let's go back to our room and wait." Barely a word was spoken, as his wife and daughter did exactly what he instructed. What else was there for them to do? They all sensed that this was surely the beginning of the end. And so they remained, sitting quietly, just the three of them, about their small table and holding each other's hands, as the deafening gunfire and barrage of screams continued unabated. "This may be our final hour," Carl announced with tears welling up in his eyes, "but there is no other way than this that I would rather spend it than being with both of you."

Chapter Twelve

From One Hell to Another

The Earth Bunkers and the outer camp fence of the Kaufering complex of Dachau.

(1945). Retrieved from http://www.dachaukz.blogspot.com

All about him, Schmuel could hear the frantic murmuring of those praying. Some, however, were by now completely delirious and shouting continuously, "The Russians are coming! They will liberate us; they'll avenge us!" Schmuel strained his neck to see what was going on in the large shower room he was about to enter. Try as he might, he couldn't make out anything. The sky was pitch black, as he, along with many of the others, waited outside, their bodies pressed against one another, as they listened to the frantic voices of those already inside. It was only when the gates blocking the entranceway were hoisted to ready the facility for them was there any light. Only then could Schmuel see into the area they were all about to enter.

The guards were yelling at them, ordering them to step forward. Schmuel's desire to survive became paramount, but he still wasn't sure there was any way he could avoid entering. Spotting a small, still unoccupied area at a far corner of the shower room, he pushed toward it and sat there, with his arms covering his head.

Of course, he knew there was no place in there where he could avoid being annihilated, nowhere the lethal gas couldn't reach. If anything at all were to be gained, it would only be to preserve his pitiful existence for a matter of seconds longer. He remained, with his head tucked between his knees, and his body pressed hard against a wall. It seemed as though his physical being was no longer in sync with his mind. Then he felt someone shake him violently.

"Get up! They are not going to kill us here!" a man repeated several times. Schmuel couldn't believe it and refused to respond. This man, a friend of his, kept repeating, "Look for yourself! Those who entered right before us are still alive. They're leaving through the gates on the other side!" Schmuel lifted his head and could see that what he had just been told was true.

"Look," his friend continued, pointing toward the gate at the far end. "They're all still alive. We've been brought here just to take showers, real showers!"

Schmuel still found it hard to believe—but forced himself to find out for himself Yes, it appeared true, but he remained apprehensive. He pulled himself up with his friend's help and proceeded cautiously. Perhaps those before him were the last ones actually allowed to take real showers. He bundled up all his clothing, which he'd been ordered to remove, along with his shoes and a belt. Then he stood right where he was for whatever was going to happen to him next.

While instinctively holding his breath, he could hear valves opening and something spray out. Then he began to feel what he hoped was only cold water on him. Still he remained mistrustful and continued holding his breath while squeezing his eyes shut. He felt his lungs burning, his blood throbbing. He felt faint. If the lethal gases didn't kill him, then surely holding his breath would. Finally, he had no choice but to open his mouth and gasp for what he prayed was air. It was—and it was enough to refresh him and pump new energy into him. He stretched his arms over his head and thanked G-d for sparing him.

"Thank you!" he said aloud. "Thank you for answering my prayers!"

As they left the shower room, each inmate was handed a pair of woolen underpants. Schmuel examined the garment and could tell that it had been made out of a tallith (Jewish prayer shawl). Given no option but to wear something he found so distasteful, he asked for the Almighty's forgiveness before putting it on. The men were ordered to return to the barracks where they were permitted to lie down on the wooden planks, which served as beds. Then, after what seemed to be just minutes, they were awakened.

This was followed by an early roll call, after which he, along with all the others, were marched off, five abreast, to a clothes depot where they were handed coats. He heard Hungarian being spoken for the first time. A language he knew, which proved a lucky break: he was able to ask for a warmer coat from one of the Hungarian Jews who were distributing them. He was given a good woolen one, lightweight and warm.

Clutching onto this coat, he and the others were ordered to start moving again five abreast, this time toward the railway. As they passed the women's camp, where Schmuel had been able to talk briefly with his sisters, his bravest, and most brazen of them, Olga, dared to leave her barrack to see him off from the other side of the fence separating them. It wasn't easy for Schmuel to spot her at first, even though she was a fiery redhead, a color closely matching her temperament, because it had been clipped down to her scalp when she first came to Auschwitz. Olga began running alongside him as he continued to march along on the other side of the fence. Olga shouted out, although it sounded not much more than a whisper to Schmuel, to get his attention.

"Schmuel!" she cried and threw a package to him over the fence, which he managed to catch. Only for a moment did their eyes meet.

"Be safe," were the last words she said before he disappeared from view.

After looking all about to make sure that no one could see, he opened that package. To his delight, there was a loaf of bread and a hunk of cheese, both wrapped in a gray woolen sweater. Shaking his head in disbelief, he wondered how she had obtained such items. He turned to express thanks, but Olga was too far away. A guard shoved him hard on his back, gruffly telling him to, "Hand it over!"

"Please!" Schmuel pleaded. "It's from my sister. I haven't seen her for six years. Please!"

Once again, Schmuel felt G-d's grace aiding him. The guard said nothing and simply walked away.

Schmuel, upon regaining his ability to think straight, advanced toward the front row of the marchers, only to realize that the group was heading right toward the crematoria. They were no more than a hundred feet away. His heart began pounding again, and all his worst suspicions returned.

"Am I now going to meet my end?" he wondered to himself in horror. He shoved his trembling hands into his coat pockets in an attempt to conceal his fear.

"Halt!" the guards shouted at them nearby the entrance to the ovens. "About face!" to which all the inmates dutifully obeyed.

The next thing they knew, they were herded toward a freight train, which they were ordered to board. Schmuel appreciated that he was once again being spared the worst of fates, although he had no idea where the cattle car might be heading. But what could possibly be worse? This train was not much different from the one that had brought him to Auschwitz; although this train, too, had those hateful buckets for human waste. They were handed food rations that had to last for three full days, although he realized that travel on such transports could last much longer. He had to make sure that what he had would last.

After the train was filled beyond reasonable capacity, Schmuel felt his car jolt as it started on its journey. The men, all standing, regained their balance as the train gathered speed. Schmuel had mixed feelings as he thought about his sisters still in Auschwitz. As the distance increased between himself from the inferno known as Auschwitz Birkenau with every rotation of the train's wheels, he felt laden with a sense of guilt at having to leave the four of them there. True, he had no control over what was happening to him, but he believed that the camp was the true incarnation of hell on Earth. Now he had to endure forever the thought of the excruciating suffering that Rose, Gizi, Olga, and Elsa had to continue to endure, something he had no way to alleviate.

As the train continued away from Auschwitz, Schmuel had no idea whether he would be fairing any better than those he left behind. He wanted desperately to believe that they were being sent to clean rubble from war-torn German city streets, and that thought kept him somewhat hopeful. He kept repeating Inge's instructions regarding whom to contact were he to find himself in Bremen. Just thinking back to his times spent with her helped relieve some of his anxiety as well as keeping him from dwelling on what might come next.

Schmuel looked forward to seeing German cities in ruins. Occasionally they could catch glimpses of the towns as they passed through in Moravia, in Sudetenland, part of Czechoslovakia known as the "Protectorate," which Hitler had grabbed in 1938. Then the train passed through Austria, renamed "Ostmark," until it eventually stopped at a place he had never heard of: Kaufering.

Schmuel had no food left; the waste buckets were overflowing, and the stench was unbearable. Although he had carefully rationed all his provisions, including the extra food from Olga, he had shared some of the bread and cheese with the others, who had been strangers when they left Auschwitz and now had grown close.

As soon as the train finally slowed down and halted at its final destination, he got a glimpse of what was outside and somberly realized, "There is nothing here to be cleared away." Schmuel found himself immediately suppressing what he had hoped would have been good fortune. Now, he would have to figure out some other way to reunite with his beloved Inge.

"*Raus, raus! Schnell, schnell!*" (Out, out! Quick, quick!) The guards shouted at the beleaguered trainload of men.

Hearing those detested words again meant that he had left one hell to be deposited into another and, without a doubt, no better than the one he had just left.

As they stepped off the boxcar, the men were separated into several groups and marched off to their new prisons. Schmuel's group was led into the third section of an eleven-section facility called the Kaufering Complex. It was a part of Dachau, the large concentration camp situated near Munich.

He had been nearly starved to death before leaving Auschwitz and then weakened further by the grueling days spent in that cattle car. The men were handed cups of a hot brown liquid, supposedly coffee, along with thin cotton blankets. Then they were marched, five abreast, off to the *Erdbunker* (earth bunker), where they would sleep from then on, which was a knee-deep wooden-lined trench, roughly 220 meters in length by five meters wide, on top of which was a sloping roof. There was but one door and, at the far end, a single window. Toward the middle there was a small iron stove. No mattresses, just straw to pile on top of the rough wooden planks that served as their beds.

Schmuel, along with the hundreds of others, were so exhausted from their journey that they all just plopped on top of the straw and immediately fell asleep. They were awakened well before dawn by icy water splashing down through the rafters. Schmuel could see moonlight coming through the rough-hewn wooden roof, as water fell on them from the melting snow. He was much too exhausted to move to avoid getting soaked. He pulled his thin blanket up over his face and did his best to put up with all the dampness for the rest of that cold night.

Upon everyone's awakening the next morning, hungrier than ever and still weak, they were ordered to line up for an *Appel* (roll call), after which they were given their work assignments. Schmuel again used his knowledge of Hungarian to obtain an advantageous job. After being handed a spade, he was directed to dig holes behind the several rows of barbed wire fences surrounding the camp, the kind of work he preferred. Not only wasn't it as hard as what many of the others were ordered to do, but it kept him inside the camp where slightly larger bread rations were generally distributed.

But even that slight advantage didn't last long and neither did the extra bread. Schmuel was ordered to join the "Sieman's Group," which, in addition to the actual work, required much walking before they reached where they had to labor. The men were kept busy moving heavy equipment and carrying machine parts for it. When it wasn't snowing, their trek there wasn't as bad because they could use the small carts they'd been given. Also, working in an area surrounded by woods and meadows was most welcome after enduring the stench and smoke from burning human bodies in Auschwitz.

As the weather grew worse, and without proper boots to walk in, the elements took a toll on every inmate. Thank G-d, Schmuel had a warm woolen coat; something others had often offered extra loaves of bread for, which he had the good sense to turn down.

Among the many indignities these men were made to suffer, they were ordered to cut two strips of cloth from the backs of their coats and then sew them, crisscrossed, to form better targets for the guards to shoot at if they became so inclined. Schmuel couldn't bring himself to damage his beloved overcoat.

He located some different material to sew on and hoped no one would notice.

The only other garment they had to wear was the thin blue-and-white-striped uniforms, and the shoes they received in Auschwitz. The soles of Schmuel's shoes were beginning to rip apart. He made the best of it, but there was no way to avoid the many pools of water that formed whenever it rained, and he, like all the others, was forced to march right through them. Making matters worse were those mornings when long formations of thin ice cracked open as they walked over them, and the freezing water beneath flowed into his shoes.

The SS guards didn't care. They just continued shouting: "Keep marching! Straight on!"

Sometimes the icy water would come up as high as their knees, and the men had to work all day long with wet and frozen feet and legs. There were weeks on end when Schmuel had neither dry shoes nor rags, which he would bind around his feet in place of socks. That Schmuel continued to believe their lot would eventually improve played an important part in keeping him going. But many of his fellow prisoners, especially those from Holland, not used to hard labor and extreme conditions, were among the first to collapse. Their deaths were followed by many among the Czechs and older Jewish prisoners from Hungary.

For those who were not already dead but no longer able to work, one or two trucks would enter the camp gates each morning after all of the work gangs had been sent out. The trucks would then load all these remaining unfortunate inmates after first having been ordered to take off all of their clothing. At that point, they were handed blankets to throw over themselves. Later that day, those blankets were always brought back to the camp, but none of those inmates were ever seen again.

It was already 1945; by then, the inmates could tell that the end of the war was approaching. Some days, when the sky was clear and the weather conditions good, they were able to see allied airplanes overhead. They looked like huge, beautiful, silvery birds, and there was scarcely ever any antiaircraft fire fending them off. It struck everyone that Germany no longer controlled the skies above them. Schmuel prayed fervently that the soil he was now standing upon would no longer remain in German hands.

"Only just a little while longer," he said to himself over and over—all to keep his hope and body alive. "I've got to survive just a little bit longer. It's almost over now."

Spring was nearing, and Schmuel had to admit that, after confronting such a harsh winter, one that had taken such a toll on him, his health was worsening. He couldn't risk not going to work as much as he felt like staying away or even to report that he was sick, given what he knew about those who had been placed on the trucks with nothing but a blanket on. The camp doctor, Dr. Weinberger, who could do little for him when Schmuel had no choice but to pay him a visit, at least gave him a piece of bread.

Schmuel admitted to the doctor to having long bouts of diarrhea, the most common ailment in the camp. His temperature was 104 degrees. Schmuel, though feverish, remained fearful of the doctor's prognosis, insisted he was fine and headed back to work. But for the first time since he had been incarcerated, he could barely drag himself through the day. He had to stop repeatedly to rest. Finally, he was no longer able to work.

That night he went back to see Dr. Weinberger, hoping to G-d that he would prescribe some treatment that allowed him to get back to work. But all the doctor could do was hand him another piece of bread. "I am sorry, but you will have to go to the *Revier* (sick room)," he said, apologetically. "You have typhus fever."

Schmuel panicked and insisted he would be fine and that he didn't have anything serious. No matter what, he had to avoid the camp hospital. The SS raided there when least expected and filled their trucks until full with those too ill to work. Schmuel tried to get up to leave, wavered, and was about to fall. The doctor quickly assisted him back into a chair.

"You have to go to the Revier. There, you'll be well taken care of," Dr. Weinberger insisted, looking him straight in the eyes.

Schmuel sensed that the doctor ought not to be trusted, although he so desperately want to believe him—he was a Jew, after all! The doctor had taken an oath to always care for the sick. Schmuel finally decided to go to the ward, saying to himself, "Perhaps he knows of something I don't."

He had to lie down at the *Revier* on wooden planks that served as hospital beds and was given no medication, something he suspected would be the case. Schmuel tried to convince the nurse in charge that he was well enough to leave, but he wasn't permitted to do so. He spent each day lying in "bed" and staring at the entrance—for which he was grateful. At least the "angels of death" hadn't come to pick him up and load him onto a truck. After about a week, on Friday, March 31, 1945, his condition worsened, and he was ordered to line up with the others out of doors to be placed on one of those trucks.

Several small hand-carts were also standing there for those to be placed in who were unable to walk and then to be pushed along by the others. Although Schmuel could hardly walk, he didn't dare allow himself to utilize one of them out of fear that he, too, would be placed on a truck and then be disposed of. Upon going out of Camp 3, to his surprise, they then walked slowly and painfully toward Camp 4 – "The Typhus Camp," arriving there about two hours later.

This was clearly meant to be their next to final destination, situated as it was near a small forest, which could serve as a burial ground. Schmuel had already heard stories of how prisoners would be taken to such places, and then just left there to die either from starvation or their overall weakened state. As the gates to Camp 4 opened, no one appeared to direct them. That, too, confirmed his suspicions that the only reason for them being there was to die.

Their food rations in Camp 4 consisted of only a blackish, lukewarm, bitter-tasting broth each morning, with a piece of moldy bread. In the evening, they were fed a tasteless liquid called "potato soup" one day and "vegetable soup" the next—

but neither contained potatoes nor vegetables. Still, everyone consumed the soup, they were all that hungry. When they asked for more, none was ever given. Some even ate the grass in the courtyard, for as long as that lasted.

There were so many patients in Schmuel's bunker, sometimes there was hardly even room for them to lie down. Every night, there were those who died, sometimes as many as five, whose corpses were then hauled away in the morning. Schmuel could recall how one night he had lain beside a Mr. Schwartz whom he could hear murmuring, "Life isn't worthwhile anymore," and then, shortly after, he had died. But Schmuel decided not to ask that the body be removed for fear of another inmate replacing him. He so desperately wanted to be able to sleep stretched out on his back for one night, even if that meant lying partially on top of a corpse. Nothing he had ever experienced was as demeaning as that—it made him barely human.

Why try to remain alive? Why not just give up like all of those others? The answer for Schmuel was simple: he was too terrified to die. He believed that were he to die of starvation, perhaps his hunger would continue to torment him even after death. He had already seen common graves where a dozen or more emaciated corpses were piled on top of one another in a single pit. How would anyone ever know where his particular final resting place was? How could his family visit his grave, or recite their prayers over him? Besides, how could he leave his brothers and sisters behind—or his beloved Inge? He had to remain alive to look after all of them. Anything he could do to help save them, he must. But what? How could anyone possibly survive all that he was going through?

Chapter Thirteen

The Gates are Opened

Photograph of visit from the Red Cross. Terezin. By Severoceske Nakladatelstvi, 1988. Image 294. Within days after the Soviets liberated the camp on May 8, 1945, trucks from the International Red Cross arrived with food and medical supplies along with a contingent of nurses to battle the typhus epidemic.

Inge and her parents remained in their room holding hands around that small table for what seemed like an eternity. The gunshots and shouting never stopped. They had no idea who was shooting at whom. They could sense the overall chaos getting closer. But their door never opened. How much longer would they have to remain in suspense? Two long hours had passed, huddled together around that table.

Inge was nervous; she wasn't fearful. If anything, she was more disappointed. Although she had survived all those years, she was thinking of the many so close to her she had lost. *For what?* For things to end this way just didn't make any sense. *What might happen to them next?* Was she doomed to wait there, not making a move, for it just to be her turn next to be gunned down? Such thoughts, after all those years of waiting hopefully for their release, made everything seem so arbitrary.

Inge realized some changes in the noise. Now there were sounds of laughter and joyous shouting. *Could that possibly be?* "G-d has heard our prayers! A miracle has happened!" she heard over and over.

Carl heard these words, too, as he got up to investigate what was going on, telling Inge and Marianne to remain where they were. Inge and her mother continued to sit there in utter silence. They were still too afraid even to voice, "We're free!" Something might still go wrong, and they would end up enduring additional punishment.

Suddenly, though, the door swung open and both women gasped. To their immense relief, it was Carl. He looked at them with the oddest of expressions on his face but didn't say a word. "Well, what is it? What have you seen? What's happening?"

Inge wanted to know. Marianne appeared too afraid to ask.

Carl just stared at each of them, as if he were in a trance. His mouth slightly ajar made it appear as if he weren't capable of forming any words.

"Vati?" Inge asked, as she felt her heart begin to sink.

She felt it would be better to know the truth one way or the other even if it only meant hearing more tales of horror.

"The Russians are here," Carl was finally able to say. "They have liberated the camp."

It was the fifth of May 1945. The Soviet troops approaching from the east were heading toward Prague on their way to confront the Germans. The SS realized that they couldn't hold out. Commandant Rahm and all his guards in Theresienstadt decided to flee. Some scattered German military units that remained clashed with the Soviet forces in the vicinity of the ghetto. But none of those who had been incarcerated in Theresienstadt were technically prisoners of the Germans any longer. On May 8, 1945, the Soviets officially liberated approximately 30,000 inmates.

Their liberators cleared out all the Germans and assumed official responsibility of the ghetto. As all of the inmates lined Theresienstadt's streets to welcome their rescuers, the Russian soldiers marched through in orderly rows along with their military vehicles. Everyone shouted, "Thank you!" and cheered them on. Music played and young people danced in the streets.

Inge didn't allow herself to join in. She couldn't understand how they could become so happy so quickly, especially considering that none of them yet knew the fates of their loved ones. She frowned, wanting to say to them, "What about all those we have lost? What about those we may never see again?" She was surprised by her own thoughts, especially after she had spent years longing for this moment. She couldn't help but feel as if those young couples dancing were stomping on the graves of the others as they did so.

For wasn't Theresienstadt no more than a way station to a slaughterhouse during those years of its existence? From November 24, 1941, until May 8, 1945, nearly 180,000 Jews were held prisoner there, and of the 88,323, whom the Germans transported to Auschwitz and other death or labor camps from there, fewer than 4,000 survived the war. In addition, another 34,000 died while still in Theresienstadt, mostly from contagious diseases, starvation, and exposure to the elements, or in the course of performing brutally hard labor.

Inge had been aware of these facts of her reality, right from the time of her arrival, but for years she did her best to repress such thoughts, to shut them out of her consciousness. In her mind, she always felt it was better to appear positive, especially in the presence of her family. Why was she feeling such despondency now, at the very moment everyone else was feeling so joyful? What was causing such feelings of sadness, disillusionment, and mourning?

One thing that struck her was the Soviet soldiers' shock upon first seeing the inmates, how emaciated they were, and what abominable living conditions had been forced upon them. The first order of business for the Russians that day, with aide from the International Red Cross, was to feed them. They had to be careful about the size of the portions and the introduction of certain foods that they might find difficult to digest. They began only serving barley soup. Unfortunately, there were those who couldn't control themselves and consumed much more than they should have and died from overeating.

The Soviet liberators urged everyone to continue going about their daily routines so as to minimize their sudden release from overwhelming them. All were ordered to be examined to determine whether they had any communicable diseases. One such test required providing a stool sample to check for typhus. Every girl in the kitchen, including Inge, who had been working in the bakery, was given a labeled glass container on which they had to write their names and fill with a specimen. Most of the girls found this embarrassing, but Inge did not flinch and did exactly as she was told. Of all the indignities she experienced in the camp, this particular one did not overwhelm her. This act also allowed her to continue working in the bakery.

But the next morning, she was prevented from entering the bakery. She had tested positive for typhus, which meant she had to remain by herself in her room to avoid coming into contact with anyone and thereby limit the risk of spreading the disease.

She spent a number of lonely days in her room— all this after being liberated.

Sign stating "Typhus, Beware!" Terezin. By Severoceske Nakladatelstvi, 1988. Image 304. To control this deadly disease, which even took the lives of some health workers, it became necessary to isolate former inmates, including Inge.

From the time the International Red Cross took over providing food, 430 liberated inmates in Theresienstadt died, and another 1,137 died during the following month, as a consequence of all the hardships they had suffered while imprisoned. That brought the total of those sent and perished in the ghetto to 35,088. Inge was struck that the horrors of the war still continued to take their toll even after the hostilities ceased. She couldn't fathom when it all would end.

Aside from receiving all her meals to be eaten alone in her room and being dispensed her medication, Inge had nothing to occupy her time but to think. She pondered what would happen to her. She was now twenty-one years old and at least still alive, but being kept isolated because of her disease that could kill others. But why was this happening to her? And why now? Such thoughts made her more depressed and increasingly angry.

For the first time in her life, she became fixated with how unfairly the world treated not only her but the Jewish people. How could people be so heartless and cruel? What was it about her, her young cousin Ruthie, her elderly grandmother who died in Theresienstadt, and her sickly mother who posed such a threat to the German people? Or to anyone in the world for that matter? And why, after she had met and fallen in love with such a wonderful man, was he snatched away from her? Everything good had been stolen from her: innocence, childhood, a chance for an education, home, friends, family members, and most of all, her first love. All had been taken because one hateful man was able to persuade a powerful nation that all of its problems would disappear with the extermination of the Jews.

As she sat alone in that room, Inge felt herself changing, turning into a different person. All that used to define her seemed as though it had escaped through that second-story window above her bed. No longer was she optimistic, or innocent, or could believe that, as long as your family was with you, nothing else mattered. Replacing such sentiments were feelings of resentment and bitterness, along with a loss of faith in humanity. How could she re-enter the world with such views? Inge was unsure if she wanted to remain a part of it. Was she truly a survivor or merely someone who managed not to die?

Chapter 14

Last Night in Dachau

American troops arrive at Dachau. The Face of Hell. By Sam Berger, 1994. p. 132. In addition to aiding the emaciated survivors, they had to attend to burying the many hundreds of corpses they discovered strewn about the camp.

Schmuel grew fearful of the night. That's when most died. It was the time when the Angel of Death appeared, creeping about, praying in the darkness on those who no longer cared to resist. Each morning Schmuel felt grateful that he was still alive. But he was beginning to find some comfort at night whenever the silence pervading the typhus camp was interrupted with blasts of anti-aircraft fire. The more frequently, the better. It obviously meant that the Allied forces were getting closer. At such moments, it made the sounds of warfare seem like sweet serenades to everyone in the sick ward. It raised Schmuel's hopes. Just the belief that he would soon be liberated helped him grow stronger.

"Only one more day," he would say to himself. *"I must keep alive until tomorrow when it will all be over."* It was the one subject he and the others talked about incessantly. While they spent hours daily discussing so many things, like escape plans and yet how impossible it would be, they were at least in agreement that the Germans would be defeated. *But who would arrive first? Their liberators or the Angel of Death?* Through the camp's grapevine they learned that Camp 3 had been set on fire. Rumor had it that all of the inmates there had been evacuated, although no one had seen any of them. *Were they actually released, or was there a last-minute frenzy by the Germans to kill off as many as they could?*

Although Schmuel didn't doubt that the war's end was near, he felt that he must try to do whatever he could to improve his chance of survival. And so, one night when he happened to overhear a conversation between two of his fellow prisoners who were planning an escape, he said he would like to go with them. But they feared he might give them away, and they threatened him. Schmuel managed to convince them that he was one of them, though it seemed absurd that he had to do so. All he cared about was saving himself.

The incident made Schmuel more determined to figure out a way to escape. First, he needed to get his hands on civilian clothes to replace the striped outfit prisoners were forced to wear. To accomplish that, he bartered his warm woolen coat. The inmate he made that deal with was more than happy to obtain such a fine garment that he even agreed to throw in a cap. It was the last great service that coat provided after having saved his life on so many occasions.

On April 25, 1945, an order was given that every inmate able to walk was to be ready to leave the camp at ten the following morning. It struck Schmuel as well as some of the others that that would be a perfect time to attempt their escape. With his civilian clothing in hand, once he had a chance to change into them, he could wander off into the countryside at an opportune moment and blend in, completely unnoticed, with the local populace. What Schmuel hadn't realized, however, was just how weak he had become. As he arose that morning, although filled with determination and courage, he found that he couldn't walk any farther than past his barrack before becoming weak and faint.

He had no choice but to remain near his barrack as he watched his co-conspirators leave. Alone then, just as he was about to take the steps he had already planned for so many days, he now had to decide what to do next. After his confederates marched out of the camp, and long after they were out of his line of vision, he continued to remain right where he was sitting. His cap still in hand, he felt like shedding tears—if only he had some left. It was then that another inmate from the sick ward, also not well enough to leave with the others, sat down beside him.

"Where do you think they are being taken?" he asked.

"I don't know," Schmuel responded. "Perhaps farther away from the approaching Allied front." "Or maybe they are being marched away to be shot," the other answered despondently.

Schmuel didn't want to think about that possibility, something that could also have been their fate. Of the thousands of prisoners still in the camp, only about 300 had felt well enough for that final journey.

Those, like Schmuel, who had to remain in the camp, were only given coffee that morning. At midday, nothing was served. Most of the SS officers had left with the prisoners who were marched out of Dachau, and, for the most part, the camp had now been almost completely deserted by the guards. Fortunately, there had been a recent delivery of potatoes to the kitchen's cellar. How starved all the inmates were, and with no guards by then remaining to resist them, Schmuel, along with many of the others, managed to get themselves up and began raiding the camp's kitchen.

It was miraculous that Schmuel was even able to stagger along that short distance between his bunker and the pantry. That potato cellar could only be reached through a small opening in its floor. Being so desperate, as well as excited by what was happening, and in spite of his weakness, he threw himself into it. He dropped with a thud onto the cellar floor. Piles of potatoes were everywhere! He took off his cap and began filling it to capacity. He even shoved more potatoes into his pants pockets. When he couldn't fit any more in, it was time for him to get out. But by then, more and more inmates had begun arriving as news of the stockpile spread. Schmuel tried to shove his way past the others, but as more inmates kept descending, some landed right on top of him.

Chaos reigned everywhere, and it began turning violent. Schmuel was frightened. He feared that not only might he be unable to hold on to his cache of potatoes, but his life. Then two pairs of outstretched arms reached down into the cellar, and someone shouted, "Come on! Be quick about it!"

Schmuel thanked his rescuers profusely. He rushed out, past the mob of prisoners still arriving, to get to the stove in his bunker. Before he even made it back there, he heard sporadic gunfire coming from the kitchen. But he didn't allow himself to turn around. He was solely focused on the feast he was about to consume if only he could get these potatoes cooked.

When he did reach the stove, there were already others who had lit a fire beneath a large pot filled with potatoes and water. Everyone there was as excited and desperate as Schmuel to get their potatoes cooked that whenever anyone newly arrived and threw a potato into the pot already filled to the brim with water, it overflowed and frequently extinguished the fire. Although the ever-growing number of inmates gathering there did their best to act rationally, they couldn't make the water boil any faster.

Their hunger increased quicker than the water's temperature. Sounds of gunfire hummed in the background. But the inmates were more engrossed with their stomachs and just kept staring at those potatoes, which were taking an eternity to cook.

"Does it always take this long?" Schmuel wondered.

Finally, their potatoes were ready, and after some arguments regarding which potatoes belonged to whom, the men finally had their first solid food since entering the Typhus Revier. So many were overly anxious to eat that they burnt their fingers and singed their tongues. Still, no other meal had ever tasted as good. That afternoon, the first in many months, Schmuel was able to sleep peacefully on those wooden slats, with the satisfaction that only having a full stomach can provide.

His sleep was disrupted when several peasant carts pulled by teams of oxen showed up. The floor of each wagon was covered with straw, and the sickest, the most helpless, and those unable to walk at all with the others were then loaded onto them and taken out the back gate into the woods. Toward evening, inmates who were still able to walk entered Schmuel's bunker, telling everyone to evacuate. They repeated their orders, but no one budged. Schmuel had no idea where they were going to be led. He certainly didn't want to meet the same fate he was now sure those taken that morning had suffered. The war was obviously nearly over, and Schmuel along with the others felt that it was far safer to remain where they were until they were liberated.

Later that night, those same able-bodied inmates returned, this time with clubs in their hands, and began shouting at them, "We are under direct orders of the SS. You must get out immediately!"

No one moved.

The kapos screamed out, "All right then. You leave us no choice!" They began thrashing the inmates. Schmuel was lying toward the far end; by the time they reached him, they had already expended most of their energy, but he still endured some blows.

No one got up to move, however.

The remaining SS guards, informed by these kapos of what had transpired, grew irate. Who did these Jews think they were disobeying their orders? Late that same night, two of the SS entered, each holding on a leash a barking German shepherd chomping at the mouth.

"If you all don't get up and go immediately, these dogs will rip you to pieces. And if you still don't get out, then we're going to set this bunker on fire!" they shouted.

Schmuel knew, given his past experiences, that such threats were usually kept. He didn't relish the thought of being eaten alive by dogs or being set on fire, so he immediately got up and went out. Most of the others did likewise.

By then, it was about midnight. Schmuel left Camp 4 through its back gate and headed toward the woods. *"Where am I going?"* he asked himself, as he stared into the dark, imposing forest. *"Should I have taken the SS's threats so seriously?"*

He stopped momentarily, uncertain as to what he should do, and heard murmuring voices. A foreign language he did not recognize. No longer did he hear any steps coming from behind him, but it was too dark to make out much of anything at all in any direction. His pulse began to quicken, and he began to wonder whether it might be better to go back and hide within the bunker. At least there he would be sheltered from the elements. He also had the possibility of discovering more unguarded food. He began walking backward, doing his best not to appear conspicuous. A voice shouted out in broken German, "You, dog, you keep going straight ahead!"

The man spoke with a heavy Slavic accent. It made his stomach sink and his head grow light. Schmuel had heard of men like these, hired Ukrainian, Latvian, and Polish murderers, paid to kill Jews in cold blood. As he turned ever so slightly, he could make out that they were all dressed in black like one imagines gangs of bandits to do. Schmuel felt he hadn't survived this long just to allow such despicable men to become the masters of his destiny. But what could he do?

He dragged his weary legs on, until he was told to halt near some railroad tracks that cut through some woods. The clearing there was packed with large numbers of sick and exhausted fellow prisoners. Most were either sitting or lying on the cold, damp ground. Many, with outstretched hands, began pleading with Schmuel and the others to help them get up onto their feet. "Please!" they cried out in different languages. "Give me a hand!" each asked. "I need to get up but can't!"

Schmuel felt ashamed not to be able to help and avoided making any eye contact. He realized that it would be the death of him if he did. He sensed that were he to assist any of them, he, too, might be pulled down in the process and be unable to get back on his feet.

Feeling hungry once again, he began grabbing young wheat and rye shoots from the nearby planted fields and chewing on them. He threw some into the sack he had with him holding the extra potatoes he had gathered up that morning. None of them knew what would be in store for them next, and there was no assurance that there would be any food. "Thank G-d for these potatoes," he said to himself, believing that they were the only reason he was still able to walk, even just to remain standing.

By the time morning arrived, a train with several cars had pulled in and slowly came to a full stop.

"Get in! Quick, quick!" the men in the black uniforms began yelling.

Schmuel saw no way to escape. If he were to try, he was sure that one of those men in black would be more than willing to shoot him in the back.

After all the inmates were forced into the cars, Schmuel was finally pushed in. The train took off with a jolt. Once more, Schmuel found himself traveling inside a cramped cattle car, like the one that had brought him to Dachau from Auschwitz. He had a foreboding that something terrible was about to happen. Perhaps they were going to be blown up. He couldn't explain why he felt that way, he just knew it. He began reciting prayers and uttering farewells to each of those he loved. He hoped they were at that moment better off than he.

Barely had the train moved, perhaps but a hundred meters, when it suddenly stopped. There was a roar overhead, and then they all felt bullets hitting the roof and sides of the cattle car. Many screamed, "It's our end! The Germans are executing us!"

Schmuel managed to see through some of the bullet holes in the roof. He made out several low- flying Allied aircraft, circling back to attack them again, shooting additional rounds of machine gun fire. A number of the men close to him began dropping, dead or wounded. He paid them no mind, as he desperately looked for some sort of cover for himself.

He sensed that, after this second strike, these planes were about to return once again. Would they hit him this time, or had they decided to drop a bomb and end things once and for all? As they came closer, the noise increased to a deafening level.

Schmuel braced himself for the inevitable. From all appearances, the Allied military were shooting as if they were targeting the proverbial fish in a barrel. Schmuel quickly voiced good-byes to family and friends. He spoke softly to Inge, "I am sorry. I tried, but I just could not get back to you."

Chapter Fifteen

Returning to "Normal"

Inge, 22, shortly after liberation from Theresienstadt.

Carl and Marianne noticed how much their daughter had changed since they were liberated from Theresienstadt. Inge's father was particularly concerned by her sudden mood shift. He felt that he had to find a way to get her out of that room. He contacted a Czech doctor he knew who owed him a favor. After having him run another test on Inge for typhus, which proved negative, they both concluded that one of Inge's fellow workers in the bakery must have switched samples out of embarrassment.

Carl felt strongly that that was the case and arranged for her to be released from isolation. Once outside, the good spirits of those now free proved the best medicine. Many at that time were already leaving Theresienstadt and returning to the cities where they had once lived. Among them were those Jews with non-Jewish spouses still at their old homes and waiting for them. To see them in such good cheer going off to their loved ones made Inge also feel that the world was beginning to return to its rightful place. But, unlike those fortunate few, Inge and her parents had no place they could still call home. Moreover, they had neither family nor friends in Bremen to return to, no jobs, and definitely no money or other assets. When a notice was circulated recruiting workers to remain in Theresienstadt to help run it, Inge along with her parents volunteered.

Inge accepted an administrative position similar to the one she had been given upon arriving there three years earlier. The major difference now was that Commite, Trude, and Gigi were no longer there. It had been quite a while since Inge had seen any of them, and she had not heard a word as to where they were now. Working out of the main building, she recorded those who had left and their destinations as well as who were still in the infirmary. Inge now felt much more comfortable being in Theresienstadt, as they were all finally receiving as much food as they desired, particularly barley, tea, milk, sugar, and plenty of bread. For the first time since their incarceration, having such items felt as if they were living in the lap of luxury.

She was also being compensated for her work. And being that they were no longer prisoners, they could come and go as they pleased. Often, Inge went with Perla, Schmuel's sister, and the other girls to visit nearby towns and marketplaces. Prague, the capital of Czechoslovakia, was but only a short train ride, and Inge, like all the other girls, would have loved to spend time there shopping and exploring. But her father would never permit her to go with them. Anti-German sentiments being what they were at the time, he feared that some of those there who heard her speaking German might become enraged and attack her.

As the summer of 1945 approached, transportation was finally being arranged for those German Jews still in Theresienstadt to return to the cities where they had once lived. Large buses began arriving to take them "back home." But Inge and her parents were reluctant to return to Bremen. Even though by the end of July most of the others had left, they felt that there was still much to be done, and so they remained a few weeks longer.

One day, when several trucks specifically bound for Bremen arrived, they knew their time to leave had come. Even then, there were some matters needing attention. Inge, for instance, who had become friendly with a Jewish couple, had left with the Katzes their son's suitcase filled with his clothing before they returned home in case their son were to return to Theresienstadt. They wanted someone they trusted to give it to him and to let him know that they had survived. Inge went to see Perla with this valise. Perla, too, had remained there longer because she had fallen off a bicycle and broken her leg. Inge visited her in the ghetto's infirmary to say good-bye.

"If their son doesn't arrive, give this clothing to Schmuel," she said. "There's a very nice suit in this luggage that should fit him."

"I will," Perla replied, all the while fighting back tears at the thought of her dear friend's departing. "Schmuel will love it."

Having hugged one another, and promising to keep in touch, Inge parted from her "sister-in-law" to board the truck bound for Bremen. Once inside, the Katz family did their best to make themselves comfortable, as they lay on mattresses spread over its hard and otherwise barren floor, the very mattresses they and others carried out from their rooms in Theresienstadt. As the vehicle rumbled out of the ghetto's gates, Inge never looked back, even though the rear of the vehicle was wide open. Her parents, too, took little notice. They were so occupied with practical concerns such as discussing where they might stay, and how they were going to pay for food and lodging. They only had a small amount of Czech currency. Inge could only think about how she would feel walking down Bremen's once familiar streets of her childhood again. She imagined that she would look straight into each resident's surprised eyes, as if to say, "Look at me. I am here. You couldn't kill me."

An older woman in her sixties, Frau Wolf, also joined them on that truck. She, too, was going back to Germany. Like so many, she had lost everyone who had been sent to the camp with her and had no home to return to and no money. She had waited in Theresienstadt with the Katzes to go back, hoping that they would be able to assist her. She proved to be a great traveling companion because everything she did made Inge laugh. In spite of losing her entire family, including her husband and daughter, she still had enough good humor left to make the rest forget their troubles.

She would take out a dust cloth and make vain attempts to wipe off all the dust from the road that kept coming in via the open back of the truck. Inge found it very funny and desperately tried to keep from laughing. This only prompted Frau Wolf to "tsk, tsk" disapprovingly and then to go over everything once again, particularly her suitcase.

Portrait of Frau Wolf taken shortly after the war.

On the evening after their first day of travel, arrangements had been made for them to sleep on the floor of a school auditorium. They carried their mattresses in with them and were treated quite well by the local residents. The following morning, after being served coffee and rolls, Inge noticed that Frau Wolf was nowhere to be found.

Everyone was quite concerned, as she was no youngster. They began searching everywhere for her, worrying that perhaps she had collapsed. Carl decided it would be best for them to split up and to knock on the doors of each house lining the street directly across from the school. Inge was particularly worried that someone had harmed this sweet lady, and she became anxious every time a door where she knocked opened, in anticipation of bad news. But then, after inquiring at about five houses, after the front door of the next one opened, she saw Frau Wolf sitting comfortably at a breakfast table with a vase of flowers on it, chipping away at a soft-boiled egg, and drinking some freshly brewed coffee.

"Frau Wolf!" Inge exclaimed. "What are you doing here?"

Frau Wolf had Inge sit down beside her until she had finished. Then, after gathering up her belongings, and thanking her hosts for their hospitality, she headed back to the vehicle with Inge.

"I just went knocking on all the doors last night until someone invited me in." Frau Wolf explained. "I told them that I had just been liberated and really wanted to sleep on a nice soft bed."

Inge couldn't stop being amazed at her travel companion's audacity. Of course, you couldn't blame her. Didn't they all deserve to get a good night's sleep finally on a comfortable bed? This just made Inge laugh and laugh, almost to the point of being unable to control herself. Inge took Frau Wolf's bag and linked her arm with hers as they walked back to the others. Inge didn't remember the last time she had laughed so heartily. Had it been weeks? Months even? It felt so good to have someone like Frau Wolf along on that trip. She was exactly what Inge needed.

Once more they traveled on and on for the next couple of days. Eventually, they reached Hamburg. There, the truck pulled into the Reemtsma Cigarettenfabriken (Reemtsma Cigarette Factory). Although Bremen was only about an hour's drive away, that was where they would be spending the night before returning "home" the next morning. The truck then pulled up alongside a waiting car, but the Katz family paid it no mind, as they began unloading their bags from the truck to ready themselves for a night on the factory's floor. The driver of that car greeted them and handed them a letter from the Bruck family.

They were that local family in Bremen that Inge had told Schmuel about the night before he was to be transported from Theresienstadt. But it had been so long since they had last seen the Brucks, and perhaps the war had changed them. After all,

Herr Bruck was not Jewish. Now they were inviting the Katzes to stay with them until they got settled. Carl, seeing their current address, noted that they were living in a particularly nice section of Bremen, the Schwachauser Ring. Considering that he had no knowledge what state Bremen was then in, or which, if any, of their friends were still there, or where they could possibly stay, Carl decided that it would be far more comfortable for all of them there than spending a night on the floor of that cigarette factory.

Frau Wolf, however, decided to remain with the truck because she was still going to travel on to Vegesack (a northern district of Bremen), where she would be staying with someone she knew. Everyone made sure to exchange addresses before saying their good-byes. Inge, after giving Frau Wolf a big hug, felt sad to see this woman leave. She had so lifted her spirits. The thought of her warm, smiling eyes and witty sense of humor served as an inspiration for Inge as she continued her return to a "normal" life.

Shortly thereafter, they arrived at the Bruck's home. Inge took little notice of where she was. She was far too absorbed with her thoughts of once again wandering through Bremen's familiar streets. Would she still be able to recognize them or would they now be completely alien? So much had to have changed during those last three years. No longer would the family members whom she would usually walk to or meet with on those very streets be there. Most, if not all of them, had probably not survived. Those streets where she had always felt so safe as a child were now going to be shrouded with her new awareness. Where walking through those streets had once given her such pleasure, she sensed that now they would be painful to traverse. When Inge was forced to go to Theresienstadt in 1942, she still had the naïveté of a child as she left Bremen wearing her custom-made suit and special raincoat in hand that she would take with her to her new "home." Now, returning, not only as a grownup, but a casualty of war, it could never be the same. She would now and forever after be the representative of a time in history that would come to exemplify the worst in human nature and the evil that lurks within far too many of us.

The next morning, as Inge arose from sleeping in a bed for the first time in years, she could now accurately appreciate how right Frau Wolf had been. Truly, there is nothing more luxurious than sleeping on a proper mattress and beneath a feather comforter. Inge had always taken such things for granted, but after sleeping on sacks of hay for so long, she could now begin to appreciate how much had been taken away from her by the Nazis. After having breakfast with the Brucks, a pleasant couple as far as she could tell, the doorbell rang, and several young American military intelligence officers walked in.

Inge would eventually become used to such unannounced visits by those in the military. Herr Bruck had begun announcing himself as a Jew as soon as he realized that Germany had lost, though it was most curious as to why he hadn't been deported to a camp. The Nazis were typically thorough in their investigations when it came to such matters. The United States troops occupying Bremen were suspicious of this family, and American intelligence was investigating. Had they been involved in any secret alliances, or had they served as spies for the Nazis? Those had been frequent occurrences. But that morning, these soldiers came bringing donuts and candies.

They had smiles and were most eager to meet the Katzes. Inge figured that they were close to her own age, at most, maybe just a couple of years older. She sensed that they smiled particularly in her direction, especially a Mr. Bird, although they were there on official business.

It appeared that, once it was established that the Katzes were staying with them, the Brucks were no longer subject to official investigation. The intelligence officers maintained their frequent visits, nonetheless. They were quite charming and helpful, and Inge as well as her parents found them to be most pleasant. Frau Bruck tried to entice Inge into taking an even greater interest by mentioning that she found them all to be quite handsome. Inge supposed she was right, but not a day had gone by that she didn't think about Schmuel and of being with him again. It had almost been a year since she had last seen him.

She gazed often at the photo he had given to her the night before his transport left, and she smiled back at his cheerful face. She also kept near the pressed rose he had given to her the night he had climbed over that Theresienstadt garden fence.

Finally feeling safe from having her belongings confiscated, she now wore the ring he had made for her for her twentieth birthday.

Shortly after they arrived at the Brucks, Inge showed Frau Bruck Schmuel's picture.

"He's quite handsome," she remarked to Inge.

"Yes and very kind. He would always give some of his food ration to my mother. Even when he had just met me."

"That was quite a sacrifice for him to make," Frau Bruck replied. "He sounds very special." "He is," Inge agreed. "I know he'll be coming back to find me now that the war is over."

Over the months, Inge would find herself daydreaming while looking out the front window of her new home, imagining that at any moment Schmuel would be bounding up those front steps, looking dashing with his blond hair and sparkling green eyes. Moreover, he would be wearing that nice suit she had left with his sister, Perla. Then he would escort her, pinky finger in pinky finger, for a long walk through Bremen's cobblestoned streets. Everything then will be beautiful and perfect she kept thinking as she held her hands upon her chin. It would be as if no time had ever passed since they had been apart—but now everything would be better, safe for them to plan a future together.

But so much time had passed since the war had ended, and still Schmuel hadn't walked up those front steps. Inge would push back from her head and heart her fear that he hadn't managed to survive. She could still feel him alive and connected to her. But it was an uphill battle to maintain that faith, especially when all those close to her were beginning to urge her to accept the worst. Carl and Marianne in particular were becoming quite concerned that she had to move on with her life, and not maintain an attachment to someone they felt was unlikely to ever appear.

Meanwhile, Mr. Bird, the American soldier, was constantly visiting, always bearing gifts and being of good cheer. It was quite evident that he was doing his best to obtain both Inge and her family's good favor. He was Jewish and originally from Vienna, which was why he spoke German so well and with no accent, and he was also already well-established in a good career. Besides, he had been quite helpful in assisting her family in so many ways. Frequently, after his visits, Inge would notice that Schmuel's picture had been turned around toward the wall. Of course, she was always quick to return it to what she felt should be its rightful position.

Frau Bruck, in particular, never ceased reminding her of all Mr. Bird's fine qualities. She insisted that Inge take him up on his offers to go out dancing. Given his many requests, Inge felt that she should at least give it a try. She hardly felt good about it, but she was tired of all the pressure. While her parents told her that they didn't want to harp on the fact that Schmuel was probably never going to come, they also didn't hide their good impression of Mr. Bird.

Inge finally accepted his offer to go with him to the officer's club the following Saturday night. But what could she wear to such an event given how little she had? Frau Bruck came to the rescue and loaned her an attractive outfit from her own wardrobe. As Inge sat in front of a mirror doing her hair, she couldn't help but approve of the image she saw of herself. "No one seeing me now could ever suspect the horrors I have had to live through," she thought. Maybe, even if only for a few hours, she could forget about Theresienstadt.

She recalled the times she had danced with the other teenagers on the top floor of the Judenhaus. They had so much fun those evenings. Maybe it would be like that again with Mr. Bird at the officer's club. It had been so long since she enjoyed herself. Why shouldn't she have a good time? Why not make up for all those years that had been stolen from her? But she wondered whether it was still possible. Could she put all she had suffered out of her mind?

There was a knock at the front door. Inge then went down the stairs to meet her date. Although she felt nervous, not knowing what to anticipate, she had to admit that Mr. Kurt Bird looked quite handsome in his uniform.

"Inge, you look beautiful," he said upon greeting her. "All ready to go?"

"Yes, Kurt," she responded, smiling. She linked her arm in his as they left for the dance.

Chapter Sixteen

Dachau's Liberators

The Liberators of Dachau.
Retrieved from
http://www.furtherglory.files.wordpress.com/2010/05/deathtrain021.jpg

Planes began to encircle the train, and Schmuel sensed that they were directly above him. Holding his breath and clutching onto his head with both hands, he waited for the bombs to drop, all the while expecting everything to become a blaze of white. He prayed that the end would be swift and painless. As the roar of the planes rose to a deafening level, he shut his eyes tightly—and then did begin to see everything in white.

"Is that it? Is my life now over?" he wondered.

No, it couldn't be. The acrid smell of the men bunched about him, many of whom were moaning, filled his senses. The sounds of the planes' engines continued incessantly, sometimes practically bursting his eardrums.

"They're circling! Look!" a man next to him shouted.

Schmuel once again grew hopeful. As he squinted through one of the train's bullet holes, he could see that the Allied aircraft were still hovering about and circling. They must have come to realize that they were not shooting at the enemy. It was the most beautiful moment he had ever experienced: German's hired killers in their black uniforms jumped off the train and ran toward the forest. The planes then flew away without firing another shot.

Here was the chance he had prayed for. Without wasting another moment, he managed to open the door of that cattle car and dropped down into a ditch running parallel to the tracks. Fortunately, it was on the far side from the camp. As he then looked skyward, Schmuel was able to catch a momentary glimpse of those beautiful silvery steel birds flying off in the distance. Grasping onto the grass, and using whatever remaining bit of strength he had in his arms, he managed to slowly pull himself toward a wooded area where he could first hide and then make an attempt to escape. A fellow prisoner approached him.

"Do you speak German?" the man asked. "Yes," Schmuel hastily responded.

"Then I'm going along with you," he answered and did his best to remain alongside Schmuel. "By the way," he added, "I'm from Romania, and my name is Shlomo."

Other inmates were climbing out of the train. The pandemonium was unbelievable. Schmuel felt he had to get as far away from the others as quickly as possible. Fortunately, he wasn't entirely lost and had a good idea of where he and Shlomo should head. From having labored at the Siemen's plant connected to Dachau, he knew that there was a road running alongside the forest that led to the village of Unter-Igling. He decided to head in that direction with his companion. They walked in single file parallel to the road and well within the wooded area to avoid being spotted by camp guards or German soldiers.

As they approached the first houses in the village, they hesitated as to whether they should go any farther. *What if Hitler's murderers were to spot them?* When they felt that the coast was clear, they chanced entering the courtyard of one house and knocked on the front door. They could hear someone walking inside. When no one answered, they knocked again.

"Please! We are hungry!" Schmuel shouted, but not so loud as to attract the attention of any soldiers lurking about.

The front door remained shut, but from a small window a woman's hand pushed out a couple of slices of bread. They gratefully accepted her offering just as she hastily shut the window.

"Thank you!" they both cried out and then devoured that fresh, soft bread, which was still steaming from the oven.

That request had worked so well for them, they decided to try their luck at other houses. But to no avail. They came upon a large number of prisoners who had just stumbled out of the woods and were noisily approaching one house.

"Oh no, this is not going to end well," Schmuel said to Shlomo.

Several of the women began running out of their homes, shouting for the auxiliary police—those who were either too old or infirm to be serving on the front lines.

"*Volksturm!*" they screamed frantically. "Someone get the *Volksturm*! The Ostarbeiter (laborers coming from the east to work) are begging. They are not working!"

Everyone realized that they had to get away from there—or they might end up all being shot on the spot. Now they not only had to worry about the men in black uniforms but the local police. Seeing a church steeple in the distance, most decided to head toward it.

"Did you hear what they called us?" Schmuel asked. "They thought we were *Osterbeiter*. They don't realize that we are Jews. I think it would be better to call ourselves *Ostarbeiter* should anybody ask."

Shlomo agreed. "Maybe that way we won't get shot if we get caught."

After crossing several fields, they hid themselves behind clumps of bushes and fallen trees. Schmuel, fortified somewhat by the excitement of their recent escape and from that slice of bread, now felt ready to deal with whatever might come next. Both men kept their ears pricked and their eyes wide open for anything at all suspicious. When they decided it was probably safe, they began making their way toward the center of the village, all the while doing their best not to attract unwanted attention.

As they passed by a number of houses, they selected a rather large nice-looking place to approach. It was agreed that Schmuel, because of his greater fluency in German, should be the one to speak. At the doorstep, Schmuel suddenly came to the horrible realization that Shlomo, wearing his blue and white striped camp garb, might give them away. But Schmuel had already knocked. It was too late now. Where could they go? What could they do? Perhaps whoever answered, Schmuel hoped, might not even be aware that Jews were forced to wear such outfits.

Schmuel looked to the heavens as if to beseech for some divine help, only to make a frightening discovery. Right above the door's entrance, in large letters, were the words, "Mayor's Residence." That meant he had to be a Nazi!

Although they both had the same idea, to run away from there as fast as possible, it was too late. They had been spotted. "What do you want?" an elderly German standing on a ladder near a pigsty and hen house shouted down to them.

Schmuel quickly reminded his companion, "Let me do all the talking. You are from Romania and don't speak fluent German."

Schmuel responded, "Good day, sir. We are Ostarbeiter. We were just attacked by enemy aircraft. The train's engine and kitchen were so damaged that all the food rations were destroyed. Until our train is repaired, we were given permission to come to this village...but told that we must not beg!" Schmuel was quite surprised, even impressed, at how good he was in making up such a story—and right on the spot.

After considering what he had heard, the man, who actually was the mayor, got down from his ladder, and had his wife come out to get her opinion—that is, to inspect them further. "Come over to the barn," said the mayor.

Schmuel and Shlomo followed him there, where he left them and closed the door securely behind him. That made Schmuel nervous, and he thought of running out from there and taking off. As he looked outside through the gaps in the barn's wooden planks, he feared that some of the Volksturm might soon appear. Instead, to his relief, a woman entered with several slices of bread, each spread with a layer of lard. Shlomo was about to pounce on it, expecting to devour it immediately, but Schmuel had the good sense to hold him back.

"You mustn't do that! Your stomach is too weak. You can die if you eat so quickly."

By the time they had finished, other Jewish escapees had also been forced to enter the barn. What was happening? By nightfall, there were half a dozen of them. It was all suspicious. "I think we should leave the barn," Schmuel said to Shlomo. "This mayor doesn't strike me as trustworthy." But as they got ready to leave, the mayor appeared, saying, "My wife is making some soup for you. Wait here."

Was this a trap, and was this soup going to be their last meal? But they were still so hungry that they decided to remain a while longer. What happened next, they could hardly believe. A servant appeared and told them all to come into the kitchen where they were invited to sit down on a wooden bench. Each found a clean plate set before him on an equally clean table. They were all served a thick barley soup containing heaping portions of potatoes cooked in their skins. Schmuel was overcome by this good fortune.

As he slowly savored his soup, the mayor began questioning him about the war. Who did Schmuel think would win? To that last question, Schmuel replied without hesitating, "We Germans are going to win the war! There can be no doubt about it!"

Schmuel hoped he wasn't overdoing his enthusiasm, for the mayor didn't seem to believe him. After asking some more pointed questions, the mayor got up and left. It was Schmuel's impression that he must be receiving some instructions by telephone as to what he should do because, every so often, the mayor would return to question him some more. Then he would abruptly leave again, as if he had to report his new findings to someone.

That night, just after eating, two of the other escapees, also suspicious of the mayor and his hospitality, took off as stealthily as possible. Schmuel and Shlomo still remained. Late the following afternoon, the mayor's wife brought them some more bread, this time with cheese. But right after that, she told Schmuel that her husband said that all of them must leave—but Schmuel wasn't physically up to doing so. Shlomo remained with him. Shortly thereafter, the mayor angrily demanded why they were still there.

Schmuel showed him how badly his legs had become swollen.

"But I promise we will leave tonight," Schmuel pleaded. "I just need to rest this afternoon and regain my strength."

After muttering something to himself, the mayor indicated that he would be in great danger for sheltering enemies of Germany were he to allow them to stay any longer.

"You see? He realizes we are Jews," Shlomo said, urging that they must leave immediately. Schmuel argued that, given with what they had already eaten that day, far more than they had received during the entire previous week in Dachau, he would rather risk staying right there in hiding and wait the war out. Later that afternoon, the mayor returned to warn them that some German soldiers would be coming and staying in the stable and barn for that night. Seeing that the two escapees were in no hurry to go, the mayor arranged for them to climb up a ladder to the uppermost part of the barn and then hide the ladder.

"Don't say a word while you are up there. And don't make a sound," were his parting words.

Schmuel wondered if he had made the right decision. *Was the mayor's seemingly benevolent behavior genuine or was this a trap?* At some point in the stillness of that night, Schmuel heard gunfire and the rattling chains of passing tanks, which shook the barn. He heard unintelligible shouting. English! The Americans had arrived! Schmuel and his companion embraced. They were practically delirious.

But remembering their still precarious situation, they decided that it would be best to remain right where they were for the time being and to remain as quiet as possible. For the rest of the night, they remained awake and sat silently atop of the straw. After a while, the shooting lessened, and the rafters ceased to shake. Even when dawn was about to arrive, Schmuel and Shlomo didn't dare to chance moving from where they were hiding. They waited with bated breath for some sign that it would be safe to descend.

That happened the following afternoon when the mayor re-entered the barn with the ladder in tow. He informed them that Unter-Igling was now occupied by the Americans. They suddenly heard the sounds of tank chains rattling past the barn. The mayor urged them to remain where they were while he went out to find out what was going on. Then he came running back, shouting, "Come help me! The Americans have just taken my son away!"

The mayor's oldest son had been at home on leave from a military hospital where he had been treated for frostbite he developed while serving on the Russian front. When Schmuel listened to the mayor's pleas for him, a Jew, to vouch for his son, a Nazi, his only thought was, "Now it's the Germans who are being arrested, not us Jews. We are finally free, free at long last!"

That day of his liberation was April 28, 1945. In spite of all that the Germans had made him suffer, Schmuel was grateful to this mayor, a Nazi, for what he had risked doing for him. Schmuel felt it was only right for him to return the favor. The mayor led him to the American commanding officer who was operating out of a house in the center of the village.

Schmuel, speaking in English, told how he was a Jew from Czechoslovakia, and that he had escaped from the concentration camp known as Dachau. He related how the mayor had fed and protected him by allowing him to spend the night in hiding in his barn. He then requested the release of the mayor's son who was so ill. The officer said he would look into the matter and then issued an order to one of his staff to see that Schmuel and his companion received clean shirts, trousers, jackets, and shoes.

They returned to the mayor's barn with those items of clean clothing. Schmuel, so emaciated by then, didn't even have to unbutton the top of the shirt to pull it over his head to put it on. They had also been given a wash basin, soap, and razors. Both discarded all their rags, never wishing to see them again. The one shirt Schmuel had been wearing now for six months was given to him while still in Auschwitz. It had become infested with lice. It had been an endless, losing battle with the vermin. Originally the shirt had blue stripes, but it turned practically all brown from the countless number of lice he had squashed on it. They placed all their old clothing in a heap that the mayor then cleared away with a pitchfork and burned.

It greatly pleased Schmuel to say to this Nazi mayor, "This is Shlomo from Romania. He is a Jew, and my name is Berger. I come from Czechoslovakia, and I, too, am a Jew." Schmuel had long been waiting for an opportunity to say something like that to a Nazi once the Germans had lost the war. Moreover, he was particularly proud not only to announce that he was a Jew, but to declare it without having to add "swine" or "pig" as the Nazis had often ordered him to say. It felt good to be able to say, "I am Schmuel Berger, a Jew," and not "AM 74" in Theresienstadt, a nameless, branded inmate in Auschwitz, and in Dachau's camps Kaufering 3 and 4, number 116096.

As evening approached, an American soldier appeared at the barn, reprimanding Schmuel and Shlomo for having gone back to the barn. Schmuel had forgotten that people customarily lived in houses. This soldier took them to the mayor's home where he ordered that they each be given a room of their own. They each had one with a view of the stable, barn, and washhouse. Because blackout measures were still in force, they were told not to switch on the lights. Schmuel was able to locate his bed in the darkness with the help of a low-wattage hall light. As soon as he undressed, he stretched himself out on that bed. At first he couldn't fathom where he then was. He was so unused to a soft mattress that he felt as if he were floating. He found himself holding onto the bed frame all through the night. In the morning, he made sure to have a good look at this "wonder bed" in the sunlight. To his shock, upon glancing into a wall mirror, he discovered there was a skeleton in the room with him—one not different from those he had lowered into common graves.

Could this actually be a reflection of himself? He stepped closer to the "reflection," and it, too, moved. As he moved one leg or the other or an arm in different directions, the "skeleton" did precisely the same. Schmuel began examining every part of himself—until finally realizing that he was actually looking at his own very emaciated self.

His naked body, which he hadn't viewed in its entirety for so long, had been transformed. Now there were only bones beneath his pallid skin, and his feet had become swollen up to his ankles. They bulged with edemas, undoubtedly the result of inadequate nourishment. No longer did he have any muscles or much flesh for that matter. His pelvic bones jutted out, and the sharp pointed ends of them were partially covered with a thin crust. He felt repugnant to look at, and he grew sick at the sight of his own body. Numerous white flakes began detaching themselves from his skin upon touch, dropping to the floor.

Overwhelmed and confused at this image of himself, he began wondering whether he might actually have died during the night while he was sleeping. And those many small flakes of dry skin falling from his body upon the slightest touch made him think this was an indication that his remains were now turning to dust. He had to know, and so he raised his gaze to meet his reflection head-on in the mirror. The face staring out at him scarcely resembled the one he could recall as being his own. His eyes now sat deeply within their sockets. They were glazed over and lusterless and left one with the impression that no life was left within them. His fleshless ears stuck out widely alongside them, while his cheek and jaw bones had become sharp and pointy. His emaciated head was now merely a lifeless skull, propped upon an equally withered neck.

He reached behind him to touch his shoulder blades, which were also covered with the same encrusted skin. Probably it was the result of sleeping on hard planks of wood for so long while suffering from starvation. Shortly after his stay in the mayor's house, Schmuel was weighed at 35 kilos, no more than 77 pounds, an alarming weight for a 5-foot-10-inch-tall man.

By then, breakfast smells from the kitchen drifting upstairs began reaching him. Brewed coffee and freshly baked bread made Schmuel's stomach respond with terrific pangs of hunger. At least, by then he knew for certain that he was still alive. Shlomo poked his head into Schmuel's room, having also smelled the food being prepared, to see whether he was ready to go downstairs with him for breakfast. The starved men devoured their food, but their appetites were so great that they couldn't be satisfied with just a single meal. Indeed, it would take many days of such meals, or even months, before they could ever get back to normal. It depressed Schmuel to think of how long it would take to recover to his proper weight.

How could he approach Inge looking as he did? Even if he managed to have enough strength to journey back to her then, the way he looked would surely repel her. No, he would have to allow enough time to physically rebuild himself before reuniting with her. He prayed that she was still alive and that she would still be waiting for him.

Later that day, after the mayor had reported for a meeting with the Americans, he returned to his home greatly agitated. Some of the villagers also showed up soon after. The largest room in the house in fact filled up. Schmuel remained sitting, just outside the door, not to eavesdrop but to catch the late day's sun. He heard shouts coming from within the room. "Somebody get a doctor! He's having a heart attack!"

The mayor had collapsed—although not from a heart attack. Probably a result of all that shock he had experienced that day. Schmuel had offered to help but was then informed by the Americans of what had transpired. The mayor, with others from the surrounding villages, had been ordered to witness the criminal devastation perpetrated by their fellow countrymen and then recount what he was shown to the rest of the population. The mayor had just returned to his home with others from that experience. Among the awful scenes were those of Schmuel's Camp 4 as well as the derailed train he had been in.

Schmuel found out that the SS hadn't delivered empty threats to him and the other patients in the typhus barrack that night they were being moved. The SS had piled the innumerable dead along with those who had been ill onto a single, gigantic heap, doused it with gasoline, and then set the pile on fire. Schmuel hoped that, at the very least, they hadn't released their dogs on those poor souls. He later learned that the SS commander of Camp 4 had shot himself in the neighboring village of Hurlach to avoid being captured. Such news annoyed Schmuel. It seemed a far too easy and merciful death considering how he and his fellow inmates had suffered.

Now that Schmuel was no longer starving, he could feel his physical condition slowly improving. But that didn't help his mental state, as he began to worry about his loved ones. He knew for sure that he would never see his parents again. But what about his sisters? And his two brothers? He felt that his brother, Wolf, had the best chance of still being alive. The last bit of information he had was that the Hungarians had sent him to a military labor camp near the front. And what about Moshe? He knew that he had been deported to the Buna camp, and Schmuel prayed that he, too, would be able to hold his own. As for his four sisters in Auschwitz, he hoped that they would be among the survivors being liberated. And, of course, he was anxious to find out whether Inge, too, had been sent there. He had told his sisters all about her just in case that might have happened. They had promised him that they would do all they possibly could to help her were they ever to meet.

All these unanswered questions and concerns began making Schmuel increasingly restless. He knew that the likelihood for even one of them to have survived was slight, but he wouldn't allow himself to lose all hope. By July 1945, the Allied radio started issuing reports that the survivors from Theresienstadt were going to be repatriated to the cities from which they came. That meant that, if Inge were still alive, he knew that she would have returned to Bremen. That, too, worried him. She was so beautiful—she would most likely be surrounded by so many admirers. She wouldn't remain single for very long. He had to get there before it was too late. If he delayed any longer, he would surely lose her forever. He was determined to leave just as soon as he was well enough. But alas, he just couldn't manage that yet.

Chapter Seventeen

Where Is He?

Inge with her father on her wedding day.

Inge arrived at the officer's club arm-in-arm with Mr. Kurt Bird, her date for the evening. They could hear the band already playing even before they entered. Many were jitterbugging. Kurt immediately invited Inge to dance, but she declined. The tempo was just too upbeat. She preferred to sit at one of the tables and watch. Kurt went to get drinks. But Inge could barely allow herself to take a sip. She was so completely taken aback by the crowd. The American soldiers had all invited pretty German women as their dates. As far as she could tell, none were Jewish women liberated from the camps. Only German women who had so recently been their enemies. It appalled her to see how quickly they could switch their allegiance. What had happened to all they had believed in? How many of those present had approved of, or actually participated in the murderous acts committed against Jews, gypsies, homosexuals, Russians, cripples, or even their fellow Germans critical of the Nazis?

These women, she thought, had too quickly discarded their former views. And for what? Cigarettes? Pantyhose? A more comfortable life in America? Inge was disgusted by what she was observing and sensed that she couldn't enjoy an evening spent amongst them. Just thinking about it was making her upset. Being seen there with an American officer by these women might make them think that she, too, was one of them. Still, she felt that she had to remain at least for a little while so as not to disappoint or offend Kurt. They left early that evening, regardless. Inge vowed to herself that she would never return to the officers' club.

From that time forward, Inge would only attend the Saturday night dances sponsored by the Jewish Community Center run by the Jewish military chaplain, Manuel M. Poliakoff. They were held in what had been an enormous residence at 17 Osterdeich. That three-story building with a spacious entrance hall and paneled in exquisite woods had been taken over to house several Jewish organizations. Chaplain Poliakoff, in his official capacity, had arranged for the offices of the JOINT and HIAS to be set up on the main floor as well as a synagogue. Both survivors and Jewish military personnel would attend the Sabbath services. Weddings, after a while, were also held there, and eventually, a great number of them were performed. So many of the survivors were most anxious to marry and to return to more "normal" existences, and to leave the horrors of war as quickly as possible. Whenever there was a marriage taking place, everyone in the community was invited to join in the festivities with the newlyweds. Kurt, who was often away attending to military matters during the week, always made it a practice to be back by Saturday to accompany Inge to the various social events being held at the synagogue.

Bremen's Jewish Community Center at 17 Osterdeich. Jewish life took root again there after the war in what was a residence requisitioned by the Allied forces.

Shortly after Inge and her parents returned to Bremen, they were given a small apartment on Georg-Groening Str. #80. Her beloved home on #33 Isarstrasse, along with Ruthie's home three streets away, were all bombed out during the war. She never could bring herself to walk those streets again. Inge's new apartment only had one bedroom, with another small room in the attic where she slept. Almost always several others were staying there as well. On such occasions, Inge moved her mattress to the living room floor, which was fine with her. Such crowded conditions were common then, given the number of Jews returning with no place to stay. Most were searching for relatives whom they prayed had survived. No hotels were operating then, and even if there were, most Jews had little or no money. Anyone passing through Bremen was always welcome to stay with the Katzes.

Soon after they had returned to Bremen, her father's cousin, Sedonie, also came back and joined them with two girls, who were close in age to Inge. One was Helga, a pretty eighteen-year-old girl with light brown hair, and Edith, from Frankfurt, who wasn't related. Edith's parents and all her brothers and sisters had perished in Auschwitz. Sedonie had become her surrogate mother. After they arrived, Inge shared the living room with them, an arrangement they all liked. Those girls were all a joy to be with.

Inge and her father soon found work in one of the offices of Bremen's Jewish Community Center. Her main activity centered around reconnecting survivors with family and friends. Her job was to contact the various agencies working to locate those to be reunited. She hoped that this work would enable her to learn something about Schmuel and her cousin Ruthie. But she never did. As the months passed, Inge began to lose hope. Then, one day an aunt, who had been living in Hamburg and, fortunately, had not been sent to Theresienstadt until February 1945 because she was married to a non-Jew, informed the Katz family that she had received a letter that Ruthie had given to a soldier. It was postmarked in Poland, and that was enough to revive Inge's hopes. She contacted the Red Cross, but it was unable to provide any further information.

Among Inge's other job requirements was to register and assist those Jews who were able to return to Bremen. Unlike what she had to do while working there before being transported to Theresienstadt, she was no longer registering Jews to enable the Nazis to confiscate their money and homes. Now she was most happy to record their information in order to help them coordinate the relocation efforts. She provided these returnees with information on various services available at the Jewish Community Center.

It also was Inge's responsibility to distribute the food received from American relief agencies as well as HIAS and the JOINT. She enjoyed that part of her work the most. Once a month survivors would come to collect still hard to obtain food items such as powdered milk, eggs, jam, coffee, tea, and blocks of Velveeta cheese—and cigarettes. Clothing, too, was available. Distributing all of these cherished items to the survivors gave Inge extreme pleasure.

After her days at the Jewish Center, her work was still far from over. She would join Helga and Edith and the other women to do the various household chores. There was always so much to be done given the numerous guests, many of whom would stay on for quite a while. Besides attending to the house, they also did everyone's laundry. Because there were no machines, they had to use washboards for everything, including sheets. After wringing each item out, they hung them out to dry on clotheslines in the garden, and then there was the ironing. Of course, they also prepared dinner each evening.

Post-war food supplies being still quite limited, the American soldiers often helped out, usually in the hope of being invited to dinner in return. Sometimes these soldiers, who spent their days hunting for Nazis still holding out in rural areas, would present them with chickens they claimed were "accidently" run over by jeeps. These casualties would be prepared as part of the evening meal by Inge and the other women. First, they'd soak them in warm water in order to easily pluck off their feathers and then singe the skins over a flame to remove any remaining down. The gift givers would typically be invited to join them for dinner.

Touring Bremen in a Jeep. Given all the attention Inge received by Allied soldiers, she was often driven around the American occupied zones of the city in one of the military vehicles.

"I don't know why so many of them always have to come for dinner," Inge and the other girls complained, as it meant that they then had to spend much more time preparing meals.

"I wish my father wouldn't always invite so many over," Inge remarked one day, not noticing that he was standing right there in the doorway.

"Girls!" he reprimanded them. "Don't ever forget about how G-d allowed us to survive as a family! Think about how lucky we are. G-d surely did that so that we would be here to help others." The girls didn't say a word. They just looked downward most shamefully, knowing that he was right. "I don't want any of you to ever forget that," he scolded, before leaving.

Life continued more or less in this fashion until one day toward the end of summer of 1945 something special happened. While immersed in her daily chores, a letter arrived addressed to Inge.

"Who could be writing me?" she wondered, as she got ready to open it. "Could it be from Ruthie?" Her heart sank as she examined the handwriting on the envelope. It wasn't Ruthie's, though it did look familiar. The letters had such distinctive shapes, only she just couldn't recall where she had previously seen such writing. She ripped open the envelope and could hardly believe what she read.

Dearest Inge,

I am coming. Maybe even before this letter arrives. Your Friend,

Schmuel Berger

Inge kept re-reading those two sentences. Over and over. She had to be sure that she wasn't dreaming. She looked out the front window to see if he might already be there. After all, his letter stated that he might arrive even before the letter. But where was he? When would he come?

He survived! Schmuel was alive!

Inge was determined to remain right by that window until he arrived. But day after day passed, and there was still no sign of him. What could possibly be keeping him away? The only one she could be sure was coming was Kurt. Every Saturday, without fail, he was there. But Inge's now waning attention began to concern him, though it didn't dissuade him completely, it did make him grow concerned. Knowing that she had received a letter from Schmuel, he felt that he had to pursue her faster—or else it would be too late.

Feeling increasingly frustrated, Kurt knew he had to act. "It's already the end of November, Inge," he reminded her, although she really didn't need him to tell her that.

"He said he'd be here before October. It's obvious that something must have happened to him. After all, the countryside is still very dangerous."

"Don't say such things!" Inge responded angrily. She didn't want to believe that anything could have happened to Schmuel especially now that the war was over.

"Well then, he's probably found someone else," Kurt argued. That only disturbed Inge even more. She wanted to tell him that it couldn't be, but she honestly didn't know what to think.

After all, she hadn't known Schmuel that well. She had heard from his sister that he had had several girlfriends before meeting her. Could Kurt possibly be right? Had he forgotten about her? Had he moved on? More than a year had passed since they had last seen one another. Too much could have occurred, especially since neither even knew whether the other was still alive.

It was then that Kurt told Inge, "I've been notified that I have to leave next month. I have to go back to America."

"Oh," Inge replied, still not entirely aware of what he was leading up to. "That's such a shame. You've been so good to us."

"Inge," Kurt went on. "I would like you to come with me. I would like for us to get married."

What should she say? Inge needed some time before responding. Surely it wasn't entirely a surprise that he had wanted to marry her. She was not that naive. After all, they had been dating steadily for a number of months now and had gone together to many dances. He was a good and honest man. Her parents really liked him—and so did she. He had been so good to other Jewish survivors as well, which meant a great deal to her, especially after all that she had lived through.

"Well, what do you say?" Kurt pressed. "Will you come with me?"

Were she completely sensible, she knew she ought to have taken him up on his offer and allowed him to whisk her away to a land far from war and destruction—far from having to see the many people everyday who sided with the Nazis, many of whom had participated in those horrific crimes. Inge had begun to take

English lessons in case some opportunity should arise enabling her to go to America. And now, here it was. How could she possibly refuse? All she had to do was say, "Yes."

"No," Inge replied. "I am sorry, but I cannot go with you."

She attempted to explain to him that, although she truly appreciated all he had done for her and everyone else, she just couldn't turn her back on Schmuel. She had to wait for him, although, as she had to admit to herself as well as to Kurt, she was probably being a fool for doing so.

Kurt left. Inge stood by her front door waving to him until he was out of sight, all the while wondering whether she had made a mistake. She prayed that she hadn't; that she wasn't committing herself to a relationship that might never come about.

That was something she kept pondering as many more weeks passed, and there was still no sign of Schmuel. Not even another letter. December came and went along with Kurt's departure. All she could do was to continue looking out of her front window and wait for a man who might never appear.

New Year's Eve 1945 arrived, and still no sign of Schmuel. Inge felt certain that he would never come. It was just too long. She also realized that she wasn't missing Kurt in the least, which gave her peace of mind whenever she recalled refusing his proposal of marriage. She knew for certain that her heart didn't belong to Kurt. A new year with new opportunities was about to arrive, and so she decided to welcome it by having some fun with her friends.

Carl and Marianne had left for a party, and so Inge, Helga, and Edith decided to throw one for themselves.

"Let's try smoking!" Edith proposed, with a rather mischievous smile.

Inge took a pack of her parents' cigarettes from a closet along with some chocolate. They turned on a radio and lit up their cigarettes. But after coughing and spitting out the foul tobacco taste, they all decided that eating chocolates would be a lot more enjoyable. Then they spent the rest of the evening telling humorous stories, dancing, and enjoying each other's company, all the while hoping that the coming year would be better than the previous ones.

The next day, they were tired from having stayed up much later than usual. Edith perched herself by the front window so she could amuse herself by watching the young military men playing a ball game in the street just out front.

"Inge!" she shrieked.

"Yes?" Inge assumed her cry was connected with the game. "You are going to go crazy at what I am seeing right now!" Edith went on, screaming out more than ever. Inge didn't think it was possible for someone to shout that loud. She made her way over to her to at least pretend to show some interest. "Don't you see? Or am I growing crazy? That must be

Schmuel! He is coming up our walk right now!" Edith burst out. She jumped up and down and threw her arms about Inge.

Inge was too shocked to move. Could it possibly be? She reached the window and looked out; there he was, walking up to the front door. How hesitant he looked just then. The first thing Inge noticed was that he was wearing that very suit Inge had left with Perla in Theresienstadt for him. He was now much, much thinner than she had remembered, and his blond hair was cut very short. But without a doubt, it was Schmuel.

There was no time to change into the perfect outfit or fix her hair properly, but she still ran to a mirror to make sure she at least looked presentable. After hastily straightening the hem of her skirt, she rushed to the door to greet him, waiting momentarily after hearing his knock before swinging the door wide open.

Their eyes met in a way that could only be described as sheer delight but mixed with great apprehension. How ought they act toward one another? It had been so long since they were last together. Each had spent countless hours praying for and dreaming of the other, fantasizing about what, if any, future they might eventually share together. But would it be, could it be?

Schmuel was struck with how beautiful she looked. It was as if all her suffering and hardship only enhanced her loveliness. "How could that be possible?" he mused. Standing before her at that moment, for all he knew, she could now be married to someone else. He didn't want to spend even another minute wondering, "What if?" and "What might have been?" Both were at a loss for words.

"Hello," they said, simply.

Remembering her manners, Inge said, sweetly, "Won't you please come in?"

Stepping aside to let him pass into the living room, she gestured for him to sit on the couch. She also didn't have any idea as to whether he still felt as close to her as he once had. The war had obviously taken its toll on him, although it hadn't diminished his good looks. If anything, those few lines on the sides of his eyes, from having lived through G-d knows what, only made him appear more dignified. Was Kurt right? Had she been a fool for remaining and waiting for a man who would no longer want her?

Inge wasn't aware that Schmuel saw his picture on the cabinet. It was that photo of himself, smiling and dressed in the overcoat and hat he had given to her the night before his transport left for Auschwitz. That was how he came to know for certain that Inge had been waiting for him all that time.

"Inge, would you like to go for a walk with me?" he asked, as he flashed a confident and charming smile.

Likewise, Inge now knew for sure that he, too, had been thinking of no one else but her during those hard and insufferable times. She looked into his sparkling green eyes and, with a smile, said, "Yes, Schmuel, that sounds nice."

Epilogue

Inge on her wedding day, June 24th, 1947

Inge and Schmuel were married the following year on June 24, 1947. It was on her 23rd birthday. Inge did eventually make it to America, moving there with Schmuel (who formally changed his name to Sam) and their two daughters, Hanna and Ruthie. They settled in Flushing, New York. Their marriage lasted nearly 60 years until Schmuel's passing in 2006. Over the years, Inge never gave up hope searching for her cousin, Ruthie Cohen, and the other members of her family. But it was to no avail. She learned that they had each been shot in Minsk a few days after Inge arrived in

Theresienstadt. But being that there was no physical evidence, she never gave up all hope. Sam's sisters and brother managed to survive, except for Moshe who died just before the liberation.

Inge's parents remained in Bremen where Carl restarted his business with the aid of an American program to assist Jews. In 1945, he re-established the Jewish Community Center of Bremen, and he was also instrumental in the establishment of the newly constructed Bremen synagogue in 1961. In August 1968, he became the president of the East-West German Commerce Association, a position he held until his death in 1972, at the age of seventy-three. Marianne then moved to the United States to be with Inge and lived to be 104 years old, also dying in 2006, just shortly after Sam.

To their immense joy, Sam lived long enough to develop close relationships with his five grandchildren and to even meet his two great-grandchildren. Marianne, with her two grandchildren and five great-grandchildren, also met her two great-great grandchildren. Both lived out their lives in good health and filled with warm friendships and close family ties. Inge, now 91-years- young, celebrated her milestone birthday surrounded by all those who love and cherish her. She has been an inspiration to everyone who knows her, and she has passed that quality of unconditional love on to her descendants for generations to come.

Die synagoge in Bremen. This synagogue was opened in 1961, in large part due to the efforts of Carl Katz, who at the time was head of the Jewish Community of Bremen. It replaced the one destroyed during Kristallnacht in 1938 and still stands today.

Acknowledgments

This book would not be what it is without the essential contributions of many others, especially the following whom I want to mention in particular.

Inge Katz, my grandmother, who trusted me with her most precious recollections of what she endured during the war years as well as giving me the responsibility of gathering into this memoir many of her most intimate remembrances of those she loved and lost. It has been both an honor and a privilege. This is also to thank her for her faith in me that I would tell her story, and that of the others unable to do so, as they would have wanted those stories to be known. You have been an inspiration to me and all of our family. Now it is time to let the world know just how truly special you are.

The late Sam Berger, whom I thank in spirit. His book, The Face of Hell, provided considerable information about his firsthand experiences in Theresienstadt, Auschwitz, and Dachau. It was his intention in writing it to bring to the attention of future generations what horrors one nation was capable of inflicting on others in the hope that his readers will become better equipped to prevent such acts from ever recurring. I hope that my efforts further his objective.

My parents, Selim and Ruth Bahar. My mother, Ruth—who has also been my staunchest supporter—has always believed in everything I do and everything I am. Without her, I would never have accomplished all that I have and most definitely not this book.

Juan Garibaldi, my husband for more than two decades now. As long as I have your love and support, I know that anything I dream of doing is possible. I'd also like to thank my biggest little supporters, my sons Sebastian and Gabriel, who use every opportunity to brag about how awesome their mom, grandma, and great-grandma are.

Helen Colman, my cousin and Inge's niece. Thank you for all of your hard work, and because of you the world will know this book. Your enthusiasm is truly unmatched.

Bill Brandon, my publisher. Thank you for taking a chance with me, and for all your meticulous hard work and belief in the relevancy of this project.

To all those family and friends I have mentioned in this book who have since passed. I pray that I have honored you, and your experiences, for all those still to come.

Manufactured by Amazon.ca
Bolton, ON